# Second Language Teacher Education

**ALSO AVAILABLE FROM BLOOMSBURY**

*Reflective Language Teaching*, Thomas S. C. Farrell

*Language in Education*, Rita Elaine Silver and Soe Marlar Lwin

*Second Language Acquisition*, Alessandro G. Benati

*Essentials for Successful English Language Teaching*, Thomas S. C. Farrell and George M. Jacobs

*Key Terms in Second Language Acquisition*, Bill VanPatten and Alessandro G. Benati

# Second Language Teacher Education

## *A Cognitive and Evidence-Based Perspective*

**Alessandro G. Benati**

BLOOMSBURY ACADEMIC
LONDON • NEW YORK • OXFORD • NEW DELHI • SYDNEY

BLOOMSBURY ACADEMIC
Bloomsbury Publishing Plc
50 Bedford Square, London, WC1B 3DP, UK
1385 Broadway, New York, NY 10018, USA
29 Earlsfort Terrace, Dublin 2, Ireland

BLOOMSBURY, BLOOMSBURY ACADEMIC and the Diana logo are trademarks of Bloomsbury Publishing Plc

First published in Great Britain 2024

Copyright © Alessandro G. Benati, 2024

Alessandro G. Benati has asserted his right under the Copyright, Designs and Patents Act, 1988, to be identified as Author of this work.

Cover design: Grace Ridge
Cover image © Rdomino / Getty Images

All rights reserved. No part of this publication may be reproduced or transmitted in any form or by any means, electronic or mechanical, including photocopying, recording, or any information storage or retrieval system, without prior permission in writing from the publishers.

Bloomsbury Publishing Plc does not have any control over, or responsibility for, any third-party websites referred to or in this book. All internet addresses given in this book were correct at the time of going to press. The author and publisher regret any inconvenience caused if addresses have changed or sites have ceased to exist, but can accept no responsibility for any such changes.

A catalogue record for this book is available from the British Library.

A catalog record for this book is available from the Library of Congress.

ISBN: HB: 978-1-3504-3816-3
ePDF: 978-1-3504-3817-0
eBook: 978-1-3504-3818-7

Typeset by Newgen KnowledgeWorks Pvt. Ltd., Chennai, India
Printed and bound in Great Britain

To find out more about our authors and books visit www.bloomsbury.com and sign up for our newsletters.

# Contents

*List of Figures* vii
*List of Tables* ix
*Acknowledgements* x

**Introduction** 1

1 **What Are the Basic Ingredients in Language Learning?** 5

2 **How Does the Language System Develop?** 23

3 **What Are the Effects of Instructional Efforts in Language Learning?** 41

4 **What Is Language? And What Is the Relevance for the Language Classroom?** 53

5 **Is There a More Dynamic Way to Organize the Language Classroom?** 69

6 **How Do We Make Language Classrooms Input-Rich?** 91

7 **How Do We Develop Communication in the Language Classroom?** 111

8 **How Do We Teach Grammar and Correct Errors in the Language Classroom?** 131

9 **How Do We Develop Effective Language Tasks for the Language Classroom?** 167

10 **How Do We Best Use Technology in the Language Classroom?** 197

11 **Frequently Asked Questions** 205

*Second Language Teacher Education Programme: Evaluation Form* 223
*Index* 225

# Figures

1.1 Key questions of Chapter 1  6
1.2 A model of second language acquisition  7
2.1 Key questions of Chapter 2  24
2.2 Lexical and formal connections in a French L2 learner's network  26
3.1 Key questions of Chapter 3  42
4.1 Key questions of Chapter 4  54
5.1 Key questions of Chapter 5  70
5.2 Support person and information finder  73
5.3 Planner and co-worker  74
5.4 Open-ended discussion  75
6.1 Key questions of Chapter 6  92
6.2 Interactive speaking task  107
7.1 Key questions of Chapter 7  112
7.2 Written language task  125
8.1 Key questions of Chapter 8  132
8.2 Explicit explanation of grammar rules (English past tense)  134
8.3 Explicit explanation of grammar rules (French perfect tense)  135
8.4 Drill practice (English past tense)  135

**8.5** Drill practice (French perfect tense) 135
**8.6** Referential structured input activity 141
**8.7** Referential structured input activity 141
**8.8** Affective structured input activity 142
**8.9** Affective structured input activity 142
**8.10** Textual enhancement activity 146
**8.11** Input flood activity 147
**8.12** Mechanical output practice 148
**8.13** Structured output activity 150
**9.1** Key questions of Chapter 9 168
**9.2** Interactive reading and comprehension task 193
**10.1** Key questions of Chapter 10 198

# Tables

**2.1** Sequence of acquisition of negation in English  27

**2.2** Sequence of acquisition of *ser* and *estar* in Spanish  27

# Acknowledgements

A special thank you to colleagues who read the first drafts of this textbook. My gratitude also goes to the BEd students at UCD for their valuable feedback on how to improve the content of the textbook.

# Introduction

The main aim of this textbook is to provide both trainee language teachers and undergraduate students with an evidence-based second language teacher education programme. This textbook responds to the demand for a teacher education programme which is not based on simply training language teachers to use textbooks. In this textbook, how the principles derived from theory and research in language learning can be applied to day-to-day classroom language teaching pedagogy will be examined. This highly accessible introductory textbook carefully explores the main questions that have driven the field of second language learning and language teaching which are relevant to improving classroom language pedagogy. The textbook can be used for teacher language education programmes or as a stand-alone introductory module/course on language learning and teaching.

All language teachers, to become effective teachers and bring innovation to the language classroom, must develop the following:

- An understanding of how humans learn a second language,
- An understanding of the nature and role of language and communication,
- An understanding of the relation between theory and research in second language learning and language teaching.

Intended for language teachers and students with little or no background in linguistics or second language learning theory and research, this textbook explains important key facts in second language learning and how/why they are relevant for classroom language teaching. The idea is to discuss, examine and propose an effective and evidence-based language teaching pedagogy. This textbook is organized around key questions so that readers can more successfully grasp the basic questions that drive the field of language learning and teaching.

Key features in each chapter include the following:

- easy, reader-friendly style with no citations,
- jargon avoided and technical terms explained in the context,
- callout recap called 'in a nutshell….' These boxes highlight the main ideas,
- boxes called 'Reflect on this…' which invite readers to ponder something related to what they have just read,
- 'task' and 'quiz' sections through each chapter,
- 'what the research is telling us …' section to summarize main research findings,
- 'takeaway' section that summarizes important points in each chapter,
- 'knowing more about the subject' at the end of each chapter,
- 'further clarifications …' section to further clarify some key terms used in each chapter,
- An evaluation form to be used at the end of the programme is provided.

The textbook is organized into eleven chapters under ten key questions and a FAQ chapter:

1. What are the basic ingredients in language learning?
2. How does the language system develop?
3. What are the effects of instructional efforts in language learning?
4. What is language? And what is the relevance for the language classroom?
5. Is there a more dynamic way to organize the language classroom?
6. How do we make language classrooms input-rich?
7. How do we develop communication in the language classroom?
8. How do we teach grammar and correct errors in the language classroom?
9. How do we develop effective language tasks for the language classroom?
10. How do we best use technology in the language classroom?
11. Frequently asked questions

# Second Language Teacher Education Programme: Evaluation Form

What are the basic ingredients in language learning? In this chapter what is known about how people acquire a language will be examined. Key facts will be highlighted to provide the reader with basic information on language learning processes.

How does the language system develop? In this chapter how the language system grows and develops in our mind will be explored.

9 effects of instructional efforts in language learning? In this chapter the role of instruction in second language learning will be discussed.

**What is language? And what is the relevance for the language classroom?** Language is a complex, abstract, implicit system, and the rules we know are not the rules we have in our heads. What language learners have in their minds is an abstract system and pedagogical rules which describe only the surface parts of the sentence but not the underlying information. This chapter discusses the nature and role of language.

**Is there a more dynamic way to organize the language classroom?** In this chapter of the textbook, a new role of L2 learners and language teachers in the classroom will be presented. Roles that must be conducive to communication and effective learning. A communicative and process-oriented way to incorporate vocabulary learning in the language classroom will be examined.

**How do we make language classrooms input-rich?** In this chapter how we can make input comprehensible and message-oriented (easy to process) in the classroom will be discussed. Examples for language learners to engage in interaction and negotiation of meaning opportunities will be provided. How to develop interactive speaking tasks will also be examined.

**How do we develop communication in the language classroom?** In this chapter what communication is and how it can be fostered in the classroom will be discussed. Communicative and composing-oriented tasks to foster written competence will be examined.

**How do we teach grammar and correct errors in the language classroom?** In this chapter different ways to provide a grammar focus in the language classroom will be discussed and practical examples provided. The role and nature of corrective feedback will be examined.

**How do we develop effective language tasks for the language classroom?** In this chapter an examination of what a language task is will be presented. Tasks can be effectively used in the classroom to develop listening and reading comprehension competence when acquiring another language.

How do we best use technology in the language classroom?

**Frequently asked questions**

In this final chapter we summarize the main takeaways about second language learning and indicate what we need to do to be innovative in language teaching.

### Main takeaways about second language learning

- Language is mental representation and not a skill.
- The basic data for second language acquisition is communicative input.
- Learners must process language making appropriate form-meaning connections.
- Language is constrained (stages and orders).
- There is a qualitative difference between explicit and implicit knowledge of language.

### To be innovative in language teaching we must

- Develop a good working definition of communication.
- A focus on form should be input-oriented and meaning-based. Teachers are too preoccupied with teaching and testing grammar.
- Instructors and materials should provide student learners with level-appropriate input and interaction.
- Communicative and interactive language Ttsks should form the backbone of the curriculum.

### Second language teacher education programme: Evaluation form

# 1

# What Are the Basic Ingredients in Language Learning?

Overview 5
What Is Second Language Learning? 6
  A Little History 7
What Are the Basic Ingredients? 10
  The Nature and Role of Input 10
  Innate Mechanisms 14
  Similarities 18
  Differences 18
Knowing More about the Subject 20

## Overview

Second language (L2) learning theory and research examines three main issues: (1) how language learners comprehend and process language; (2) how the internal language system develops; (3) how language learners tap into that system to produce language. A distinction is often made between the first and the second language. The second language (L2) is the language learned after the first language (L1) which is acquired in early childhood. Researchers have investigated the processing and linguistics processes and constraints associated with learning a language. In this first chapter, you will explore two main questions (Figure 1.1 below): (1) What is L2 learning?, (2) What are the basic ingredients in language learning?

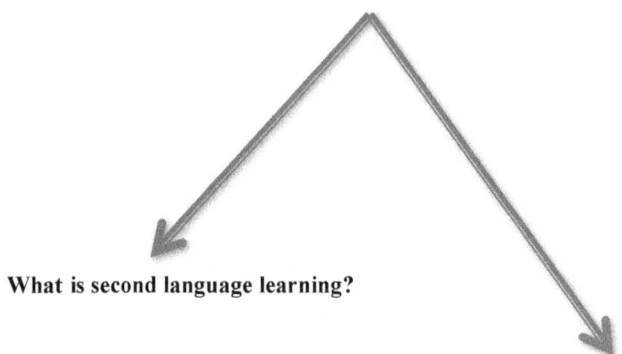

What is second language learning?

What are the basic ingredients in language learning?

**Figure 1.1** Key questions of Chapter 1.

# What Is Second Language Learning?

The study of L2 learning addresses three fundamental questions:

(1) How is the second language we are exposed to in the input processed?
(2) How does the second language develop into a system?
(3) How do language learners make use of the language system?

The progress made in understanding language learning can be equated with the completion of a puzzle. We have all the pieces on the table and we have made significant advances in piecing them together but the job is not finished and the puzzle is not completed yet. Despite requiring more work, there are several key facts in L2 learning we can all agree with.

> ### Reflect on This ...
>
> Before you begin reading about the object of L2 learning theory, take a minute to explore what you already know about how people learn a language.
>
> What do you know?
>
> Where do your ideas come from?
>
> Why should language teachers – or anyone – study how we learn a second language?

INPUT → INTAKE → LANGUAGE SYSTEM → OUTPUT

**Figure 1.2** A model of second language acquisition.

Learning a second language entails the acquisition of different systems (e.g. words, sounds, syntax). Words in a language carry meaning and sounds, and language learners must create a mental network linking each one to another. For example, the word *singer* carries the meaning of a person who sings, a specific sound '/sɪŋə(r)/', it is linked to the verb *to sing*, and to the noun *song*. Syntax deals with the location and movement of words in a sentence, the so-called sentence structure. For example, the sentence *I watch TV* in English is possible, but *I TV watch* is not allowed. This is because English has a word order structure called SVO (Subject-Verb-Object) which is required to be followed when we string elements such as an object and a subject in a sentence for language use. Language learning consists of several mechanisms and processes which are responsible for the following: how language learners process input, how their language system grows and how eventually language learners make use of the language for speech production. A model of L2 learning (Figure 1.2) is characterized by at least the following four main components.

Later on in this chapter these components will be described.

# A Little History

Behaviourism was a theory in the 1940s and 1950s which maintained that human learning is about imitating good behaviours. Language was seen as a progressive accumulation of habits and the goal was error-free production. These assumptions were consistent with the beliefs that language learners should go through extensive drill and practice as language is learned by imitating correct behaviour. The first language (L1) was seen as a major obstacle to L2 acquisition since it caused interference errors (caused by habits in the L1) and negative transfer (from L1 to L2) of habits. Theorists believed that language learning proceeded from form to meaning (first master the grammatical forms and then move on to express meaning). This theory was translated into a language teaching method called Audiolingual Method. This method suggested that language teaching should focus on rules learning, language memorization, repetition and drill practice.

In opposition to this view was the innate position which argued that a child starts with a knowledge of language universals and generates from that knowledge a series of hypotheses about the particular language s/he is learning, at the same time modifying and correcting the language system in the light of the data available. According to the innate view, language learning can't be treated as a process of mechanical habit formation. Instead the idea is that language learners already possess an in-built hypothesis-forming device (an internal and universal language structure in the mind) and the teacher's role is reduced from that of structuring the learning path to presenting the 'linguistic data' which the language learners react to and manipulate to develop their internal language system.

The question raised by scholars at that time was: How do language universals in child language acquisition affect adult language learning? Some researchers claimed that the same universals that children use to construct their native language are available to adults. Some empirical research carried out in the 1960s/1970s lent support to the view that adult L2 learning was no different from child L1 acquisition. These findings were a stimulus for researchers to look for evidence of similar processes in L2 learning. They found similarities in two main areas: in the sequences that emerge when adults and children learn an L2 in a natural setting and in the kinds of errors that adult learners make in the classroom. Researchers drawing on L2 research emphasized the role of the learner and began to make very radical proposals about syllabus design and classroom methodology. It was suggested that language learning should be allowed to take place naturally in the course of using the L2 for communication. Naturalistic L2 learning was seen as a model of successful learning, and the goal of language pedagogy was to reproduce the conditions that made it successful.

In the 1970s, a new word was coined: 'interlanguage'. This term described the existence of a linguistic system evidenced when language learners use the second language in the process of learning it. The interlanguage system is very organized and grows as we process more language and we accommodate more words in the system as we make successful word-meaning mappings.

The 1980s marks the importance of the use of language in real situations to perform authentic communicative functions. It was recommended a return to a natural approach where classroom learning has to closely resemble naturalistic L2 learning. The so-called Monitor Theory argued that the way children develop their L1 and the way adults learn an L2 are similar.

There is a need for the creation of a kind of environment in an L2 classroom that resembles the condition where L1 learning takes place. It was hypothesized that if L2 learners were exposed to 'comprehensible' input and were provided with opportunities to focus on meaning and messages rather than grammatical forms and accuracy, they would be able to acquire the L2 in much the same way as L1 learners. There are certain practical implications for classroom practice consistent from this view which form the basis of the Natural Approach and the Communicative Language Teaching Approach. The two teaching approaches emphasized the importance of exposing language learners to comprehensible and meaningful input, the use of language for communicative purposes and in spontaneous situations.

The 1990s saw the emergence of a number of contemporary theories which have shaped the field: (1) input processing, (2) processability and (3) interaction hypothesis. Input processing's basic idea was that language learners bring processing strategies for making form-meaning connections to the task of comprehension. Features of language such as words make their way to the language system if a word-meaning connection is made. However, only part of the input is processed (intake) due to language processing constraints. Processability theory's main concern was to investigate the constraints on learner production of formal features during real-time communication. The outcome of this research demonstrated that language learners follow stages to access information in the language system for speech production. The interaction hypothesis was developed with the view that comprehensible input is a key factor in L2 learning, and the research associated with this theory focused on how input can be made comprehensible. Interaction referred to conversations between the language learner and other interlocutors. The Interaction hypothesis focused on how such interactions might affect language learning by positing that interactions play a central role in learning languages. Language learners should be provided with genuine opportunities for communication.

In recent years, the field of L2 acquisition is largely focused on the mind/brain. From a psycholinguistics and neurolinguistics perspective, more sophisticated methodological tools have been used to carry out research in L2 learning in an attempt to measure implicit knowledge and how language learners process language. Language learning is implicit in nature and implicit knowledge is unconscious and not intentional knowledge.

## Reflect on This ...

If you would like to know more about the history of second language research and theories, please read VanPatten, B., Smith, M., &

> Benati, A. (2020). *Key questions in second language acquisition: An introduction.* Cambridge: Cambridge University Press (chapter 1).

# What Are the Basic Ingredients?

## The Nature and Role of Input

> **In a Nutshell ...**
>
> Input is the essential element in language learning. It is the language we hear or read and it carries a meaning.

In the model of language learning previously displayed, what is input? Input can be defined as the language learners hear or read which carries a specific message. Language learners must comprehend the language they hear or read and this involves being able to extract meaning from the input.

No successful learners acquire a language without input and all aspects of language are input dependent (e.g. lexicon, morphology, phonology, syntax).

Input, aural or written, provides the raw data for our internal mental processors to develop the new language system. Input is successfully comprehended if learners can make an accurate mapping between words and meanings. For example, they need to be able to link the word *cat* with the meaning of a feline with four legs. Words are learned in context. The main bulk of vocabulary happens through comprehension, and vocabulary leads to the acquisition of grammar because individual words carries meaning and grammatical properties.

Input is an essential ingredient for language learning and must have two characteristics to be successfully comprehended and processed into our language system: (1) it must be comprehensible to the learner, (2) it must convey a clear message which needs to be attended by the learner. To make input easy to be comprehended by language learners it needs to be linguistically simplified. To make it simpler to comprehend and process, language teachers should consider the following:

- expose language learners to familiar vocabulary or vocabulary that is frequent in the target language;
- use slow and clear speech;
- make use of simple and short sentences which are easy to understand;
- expose language learners to comprehensible and meaningful input using non-linguistic means (e.g. pictures, cartoons and use of gestures).

More on how we can make the language classroom input-rich in Chapter 4 of this textbook.

## Reflect on This …

Which of the following examples is input conducive to language learning?

A. My friend loves Italian cinema. He particularly likes Fellini's films …
B. The past tense in English is formed by adding -s to the stem of the verb …
A) *Mi amigo le encanta el cine italiano. Le gustan las películas de Fellini, Rosi y Amelio. Mañana vamos a ver la última película de Sorrentino.*
B) Le passé composé est composé de deux éléments: le présent d'un verbe auxiliaire (soit avoir ou être), suivis par un participe passé.

Can you make an example of good input for learning in another language?

Unfortunately, not all the input we hear or read enters our language system. The input is filtered (processed) by language learners who unconsciously make use of strategies to cope with the information they need to comprehend when learning a second language. The result of this is the reduction of the input that makes its way into the language system. The reduced input is called intake. For example in the sentence *Yesterday, Paul watched*

## In a Nutshell …

Language learners must be exposed to comprehensible and meaningful input.

> **In a Nutshell ...**
>
> Intake refers to the language data which is actually comprehended and processed by language learners.

TV with Anna, learners will first process the word 'Yesterday' before the verb 'watched' making a word connection that refers to an action in the past (Yesterday = the action that happened in the past). In this way, the language processed is reduced and limited to the processing of the lexical item (the word 'Yesterday') in the sentence missing out the form *-ed* which also encode pastness.

Intake refers to the language data that is actually processed by language learners and there are several factors responsible for the fact that not all the input turns into intake:

- all humans have a limited capacity of processing information. Our so-called working memory system (a space in our mind where information is stored before it is transferred into our language system) has limited capacity for processing information, and when it is full, individuals need to wait until the information received is fully processed (transferred into the language system) before allocating more attention to the language we are exposed to and being able to store further information;
- all humans process information in the form of form-meaning connections. What it means is that one form (past tense form, *ed* for example) must be connected to the concept of an action that has already taken place (action in the past) to be fully processed and pushed into our language system. This process is unconscious and implicit;
- all humans possess internal implicit strategies to cope with the amount of input they are exposed to. These internal strategies allow language learners to select and process the information they receive. As in the previous example provided, language learners tend to process familiar words before verb features when both express the same semantic information (*Last night I watched football*). In the sentence in brackets, learners would tend to process the lexical item (*Last night*) first before the verb item (*-ed* verb ending) as they both encode the same meaning (semantic information).

The role of input in L2 learning has been considered from a number of perspectives which have the following commonality: input is a key and basic ingredient in language acquisition. Only a small fraction

> **In a Nutshell ...**
>
> The use of implicit processing strategies is a constraint in language learning.

of the input we are exposed to is internalized into our language system. When we try to understand the meaning of a word (car) or a form (plays), a form-meaning connection is established. For example, *ato-* at the end of the verb stem in Italian means that an action takes place in the past tense. Developing learners' competence to map a word to its meaning is essential to language learning. However, as previously said, this exercise is somewhat limited as learners filter the information using processing strategies to help them cope with the amount of information they receive. Learners unconsciously use two main strategies to cope with the input they are exposed to and select what to pay attention to: (1) they pay attention to word meaning before grammatical notions; (2) they assign the subject role to the first element they encounter in a sentence.

The so-called emergent perspective argues that input plays a key role in language learning in terms of providing multiple cues for learners. Learning proper form-meaning connections is driven by several factors, most of which are related to the reliability of a particular signal. The following factors are two of the key elements: (1) frequency and (2) reliability.

(1) Frequency refers to how often a form-meaning connection occurs in the input. If it is frequent, the signal is strengthened and students can rely on it. (2) In terms of reliability, some prompts are more reliable than others in helping learners make a correct interpretation. Language learning occurs when language learners create associations and these associations gradually grow to form a sort of linguistic network (e.g. the word game is connected to the verb to play in its various forms and tenses (played, played, game etc.) and both are associated with the word player).

Lack of knowledge of what input really is in language learning leads to misleading claims/statements and misunderstandings:

- the claim that all the language we are exposed to can be understood;
- the claim that practising language mechanically helps language learning;
- the statement that knowing the grammar rules makes language learning easier.

Interactive input refers to input received during interaction in which there is some type of communicative exchange involving the learner and at least one other person (e.g. a conversation between two or more individuals or a class discussion). In an interaction, language learners can negotiate the meaning and make some changes to the conversation. This means that conversations and interactions can make language features salient to the learner, and negotiation of meaning can facilitate language learning. Non-interactive input refers to the type of input that occurs in the context of non-reciprocal discourse and learners are not part of an interaction (e.g. an announcement at a train station is non-interactional). Conversational interaction and negotiation of meaning can facilitate language learning. In an effort to facilitate understanding, one person may ask the other to modify and simplify the language used. Interaction can be defined as a situation where there is some kind of communicative exchange between the learner and at least one other learner or the language teacher. Through these exchanges, students have the advantage of being able to negotiate meaning and make some conversational adjustments to understand the language. For example, learners sometimes ask for clarifications if they don't understand the meaning of the language they are exposed to.

> ### Reflect on This ...
>
> Think of a complete answer to these questions:
>
> If the input is to be understandable and contains meaning for the learner to understand, what is a good example?
>
> Think of some common tasks in language classrooms, such as memorizing lists of grammar words. Is it a good input for students? Why or why not?

## Innate Mechanisms

All humans possess some universal linguistic principles. This means that they would have a universal grammatical structure that resides in the mind and operates unconsciously with language. For example, in the case of question formation, they possess a specific structure that tells them what is possible (*Who do you want to invite tonight?*) and what is not possible (*You want who* to invite tonight?). This innate property we possess is called the '*poverty of the stimulus*'.

*The poverty of the stimulus* is a situation in which we come to know more than what we could have gained from exposure to the language. This concept is traceable back to the Greek philosopher Plato who questioned the relationship between knowledge and experience. Plato wanted to know how it is that a person could come to know something that was never learned explicitly. As part of his reasoning, he concluded that people must be born with innate ideas or at least some innate knowledge. In language learning, this concept means that people come to have an underlying knowledge of language greater than what the input data should have allowed them to have. The main theory that results from this view is that people are born with an innate specification for language and that certain principles about language come hardwired in their heads at birth.

> **In a Nutshell ...**
>
> Universal Grammar is a system that encompasses abstract and innate elements.

> **Reflect on This ...**
>
> Other than biology, what factors might be related to the success of children compared to adult language learners? Write down any you can think of as well as any that you come across as you read.

The existence of innate mechanisms of language learning refers to the idea that children combine biologically gifted abstract knowledge from birth with the task of learning a first language, and this abstract knowledge constrains the shape of the target language system they learn. Although the position is almost universally accepted in L1 learning, a key question in L2 learning remains as to whether the innate knowledge children have for L1 learning is still available for L2 learning, and up to that point, the learning of L2 is similar to that of L1.

The main idea is that children don't come to the task of acquiring language out of thin air. That is, children are not blank printouts upon which linguistic data is imprinted. They are not little imitators who just repeat what they hear around them. Instead, children are seen as active creators of a linguistic system and are guided by an innate knowledge called Universal Grammar in shaping up their internal language system. This means that children are born with Universal Grammar as part of their biological make-up. The human species in general have a special and biologically determined system for language, different from other systems. Universal Grammar consists of a cognitive system that contains a set of abstract knowledge and procedures common to all languages. For example, there are universal principles that link the formation of sentences. Children of different native languages learn words in isolation before they can join them into sentences and not vice versa.

Universal Grammar also includes parameters which are a component that encodes the various variations between different languages. For example, the so-called head parameter considers the verb as 'head'. In Italian, the verb precedes the compliment (*Gaia has a beautiful car*) while in the Japanese language, the verb follows the compliment (*A beautiful car Gaia has*). In a second example, the 'null subject parameter' refers to the fact that verbs can appear without an explicit or overt subject, and the sentence is not grammatically incorrect. For example, in Italian 'I speak' and 'speak' are allowed grammatically. In English, however, such phrases are prohibited: 'speak' and 'speaks'.

> **In a Nutshell ...**
>
> There are different views on whether learners have access to the Universal Grammar.

In short, languages vary in whether they allow null subjects or not, and linguists speak of a parameter set in one way or another with respect to different languages. Italian, for example, is a language with a null subject and therefore has the parameter set to '+ null subject'. English is not a language with the presence of the null subject parameter and has the parameter set to '−null subject'. The question is whether or not learners can 'reset' parameters from one value to another. In the case of the transition from Italian to English, for example, the learner should reset from '−null subject' to '+ null subject'. Parameter reset occurs when input data interacts with the Universal Grammar. The child's input is represented by listening to the dialogues of the adult which sets the learning mechanism in motion. Input alone is not enough to develop language learning. A primary role is assigned to the innate mechanisms that actively interact with the input.

Under normal conditions, all children learn their mother tongue without too much effort and without receiving any kind of formal instruction. Universal Grammar is the mechanism (special language learning device) that guides them in their learning. This mechanism is made up of innate general principles of language and is applicable and common, as we have said, to all languages. This innate knowledge allows children to discover the rules of their own language system. Children are successfully learning their native language at a time in life when they would not be expected to learn such a cognitively complicated function. The question we ask ourselves is: How can one explain the fact that it is extremely difficult to learn it? Do adults have access to the same abstract and innate mechanisms as children?

> **Reflect on This ...**
>
> Does it mean that when we learn a language with a different parameter setting, we need to change the parameter of our first language to learn a second language?
>
> Would you be able to provide an example for English L1 learners learning another language?

There are three possible views on this point (assessability to innate knowledge and mechanisms):

1. Learning a second language is fundamentally different from mother tongue learning. L2 learners do not have access to the abstract and innate devices of language;
2. Learning a second language is similar to learning the mother tongue. L2 learners have full access to the abstract and innate devices of language;
3. L2 learners transfer a limited portion of their mother tongue into language in the learning of a second language. Learners have partial access to the abstract and innate devices of language.

Experimental research on morphemes (see Chapter 2) shows that learners of different native languages seem to acquire linguistic forms in a predetermined and natural order. L2 learning is considered to be very similar to mother tongue learning in that both are processes in which language learners develop unconscious hypotheses about the language based on the input they receive.

> **In a Nutshell ...**
>
> In essence the processes involved in acquiring the mother tongue and the second language are similar.

Language learning is a process driven by innate mechanisms that are impervious to external influences such as grammar teaching and corrective feedback (more later on in this book).

The question of whether mother tongue and L2 learning are similar or different is a key question in the study of how we acquire a language. Scholars suggest that there are similarities and some differences between L1 and L2 learning.

## Similarities

1. Learners follow natural orders in acquiring morphemes.
2. The input has a primary role, as long as it is understandable for the learner and contains a message. Potential differences can only be attributed to external factors such as the quantity and quality of inputs learners receive.

## Differences

1. Children have full access to innate abstract mechanisms. Adults, on the other hand, may not have access to the same mechanisms.
2. Adults are not exposed to the same quantity and quality of input.
3. Context plays an important role. While it is possible to learn a second language in various contexts, the learning of the mother tongue only occurs in a natural context in which the child is growing up. In this context, the child receives simplified and understandable input.

> **What the Research Is Telling Us ...**
>
> - Input plays a primary role.
> - Input does not enter the mind/brain in toto. Only a small proportion of input is processed (intake). Input gets processed and turn into intake (word-meaning connections).

- In acquiring their first language, children have full access to innate mechanisms. In short, processing mediates between the input and learners' internal mechanisms.
- Adults, however, may not have access to the same mechanisms when learning a second language.
- The processes and mechanisms responsible for language learning are similar.
- Potential differences between learning a first language and learning a second language can only be attributed to external factors such as the quantity and quality of input received.
- In acquiring a second language, adults are not exposed to the same amount and quality of input.

**Task:** Please look at the following statements about L2 acquisition and indicate whether you agree or disagree.

|  | Agree | Disagree |
|---|---|---|
| Languages are acquired through imitation | | |
| L1 and L2 learning are fundamentally different | | |
| Language learning is intake-dependent | | |
| Input plays a fundamental role in language learning | | |
| Adults have access to Universal Grammar | | |

**Task:** In this chapter, it has been advocated that input plays a crucial role in L2 learning and that learners need to have lots of opportunities to work with input in the classroom. Please highlight three reasons why this is important:

- 
- 
-

> **Takeaways from This Chapter**
>
> - Input (comprehensible and meaningful) is indispensable in language learning.
> - Input must be comprehensible and meaningful.
> - Humans have an internal innate grammar system.
> - Only a small portion of input is processed (intake) by language learners.
> - L1 and L2 learning have similar characteristics.

# Knowing More about the Subject

Benati, A. (2014). Second language acquisition. In C. Fäcke (ed.), *Language acquisition* (pp. 179–97). Mouton de Gruyter.

Chomsky, N. (1965). *Aspects of the theory of syntax*. MIT Press.

Ellis, N. (2009). Optimizing the input: Frequency and sampling in usage-based and form-focused Learning. In M. Long & C. Doughty (eds.), *Handbook of second language acquisition* (pp. 63–103). Blackwell.

Gass, S. M., Behney, J., & Plonsky, L. (2013). *Second language acquisition: An introductory course*. Routledge.

Keating, G. (2018). *Second language acquisition. The basics*. Routledge.

Krashen, S. D. (1982). *Principles and practice in second language acquisition*. Pergamon Press.

Lichtman, K., & VanPatten, B. (2021). Was Krashen right? Forty years later. *Foreign Language Annals, 54,* 283–305.

Morgan-Short, K. (2021). Considering the updated Input Hypothesis from a neurolinguistics perspective: A response to Lichtman and VanPatten. *Foreign Language Annals, 54,* 324–30.

Piske, T., & Young-Scholten, N. (2009). *Input matters in SLA*. Multiligual Matters.

VanPatten, B., & Simonsen, R. (2022). *Language acquisition in a nutshell*. American Council on the Teaching of Foreign Languages.

VanPatten, B. (2017). Situating ISLA: Facts about SLA. *Instructed Second Language Acquisition, 1,* 45–60.

VanPatten, B., & Benati, A. (2015). *Key terms in second language acquisition*. Bloomsbury.

VanPatten, B., & Williams, J. (2015). *Theories in second language acquisition*. Lawrence Erlbaum.

VanPatten, B., Smith, M., & Benati, A. (2019). *Key questions in second language acquisition*. Cambridge University Press.
White, L. (2003). *Second language acquisition and universal grammar*. Cambridge University Press.

# Further Clarifications

In this section, we aim to further clarify some of the terms or concepts presented in the chapter.

**Form (word)-meaning connection** refers to relation between a form or a word and its meaning. For instance, the word *cat* is a word which refers with an animal with four legs, paws, claws, fur, whiskers and the like. The verb ending *-ed* in English is a form that encodes the meaning 'pastness' (or 'not present').

**Input** is the language that language learners are exposed to.

**Intake** is the language that language learners actually takes in (processed),

**Lexicon** is the word linguists use to refer to the mental dictionary we all carry around in our heads.

**Morphology** is the word linguists use to refer to the characteristics of words and how words are formed.

**Parameter** is a particular syntactic variation of a feature. For example, in English a subject is allowed before the verb 'I watch TV'. In other languages this is prohibited.

**Phonology** is the word linguists use to refer to words' sound system.

**Poverty of the stimulus** refers to the fact that humans have an underlying knowledge about language. They know more than what they get from the input. For example, they come to know what is allowed and disallowed from a language.

**Processing** refers to one important process in language learning: input processing. This refers to the input that learners process (called intake) when exposed to language. For the language to be processed a form-meaning connection must be made.

**Syntax** is the word linguists use to refer to the good use of language in terms of whether or not a sentence is fine and well-formed.

**Universal Grammar** refers to a linguistic theory in L2 learning which asserts that all humans have an in-built system of language since birth. This system consists of linguistic abstract principles which govern language.

The input to which language learners are exposed triggers some of these innate principles in complex interactions which results in language learning.

**Working memory** refers to the processing space where information processed by L2 learners are initially stored before further processing takes place. Humans have limited capacity in processing information and therefore a limited amount of information is stored in working memory.

# 2

# How Does the Language System Develop?

Overview  23

What Are the Roles of Explicit and Implicit Knowledge in Language Learning?  24

   Two Competitive Models  24

   Natural Orders and Learning Stages  25

   The Centrality of Implicit Learning  29

   Explicit Knowledge Does Not Turn into Implicit Knowledge  31

What Is the Nature and Role of Output in Language Learning?  35

Knowing More about the Subject  39

## Overview

A distinction should be made between language as a skill and language as a special and complex system (more on Chapter 4). How the language system grows and develops in our mind is explored in this chapter emphasizing the centrality of the role of impact knowledge in language development. In this chapter, you will explore two main questions (Figure 2.1): (1) What are the roles of explicit and implicit knowledge in language learning?, (2) What is the nature and role of output in language learning?

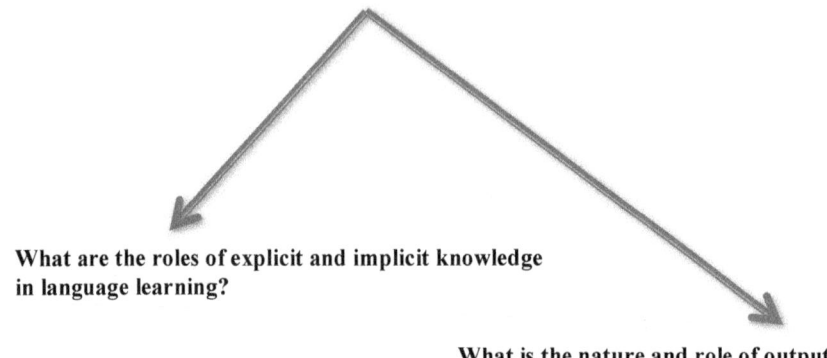

**What are the roles of explicit and implicit knowledge in language learning?**

**What is the nature and role of output in language learning?**

**Figure 2.1** Key questions of Chapter 2.

# What Are the Roles of Explicit and Implicit Knowledge in Language Learning?

## Two Competitive Models

Input is the basic and necessary ingredient for learning a second language. However, there is considerable debate over the nature, design and function of the internal mechanisms of our language system. There are two competing views about language: (1) the domain-general view and (2) the language-specific view.

> **In a Nutshell ...**
>
> There are two competing views explaining the mechanisms of our language system:
>
> - Solving problem view (domain-general mechanisms)
> - Mental view (language-specific mechanisms)

Supporters of the first view argue that language is like any other skill in life. Learning a language is very much like learning how to play tennis, drive a car and, more generally, solve problems. According to this view, language is learned via the so-called domain-general mechanisms. These mechanisms enable language learners to learn how to accurately perform a skill.

Other scholars and researchers contend that language is a special mental function and the result of complex interactions of principles. It is not simply a skill and it is not learned in the same way skills are learned. Language is a complex, implicit and abstract system, and we have specific language mechanisms responsible for developing language. Language does not consist of pedagogical rules (see Chapter 4).

We talk about the learning of rules and the testing of rules. Examples from some research:

- learning the 'passive rule'
- learning 'question formation rules'
- learning the 'rule for subject-verb agreement'
- learning 'rules for the subjunctive'

To be sure, the surface phenomena we talk about as 'rules' are real, but what exists in the mental representation are not the rules we use to describe what we see! Language learners do not internalize rules. Language is an implicit system comprising a vast network of forms and lexical items. It is like a network of lexical entries that encode both meaning and grammatical information. Lexical items linked to each other through connections demonstrating:

- semantic relations
- lexical relations
- formal relationship

The network grows in our heads as we process more language and make the right connections! In the example below you can see how different words can be semantically, lexically and formally connected (see example in Figure 2.2).

## Natural Orders and Learning Stages

Language learners' internal language system is built from input data and innate linguistic

### In a Nutshell ...

The two main ingredients responsible for the developing of our language system are:

- input a Universal Grammar principle.
- The language system is implicit and abstract in nature.

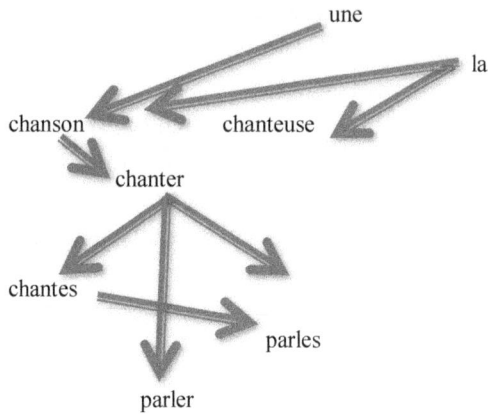

**Figure 2.2** Lexical and formal connections in a French L2 learner's network.

principles. The main characteristic of this system is that it is implicit and abstract in nature. The system is dynamic and changing, as the learner is attempting to develop a language system resembling the one of a native speaker. In our language system data is organized systematically by connecting words semantically (e.g. sad and happy), formally (e.g. interesting and interested), lexically (e.g. boring and bored) and syntactically (e.g. following SVO structure = Subject-Verb-Object). How does our language system develop? The development of the language system is staged-like and ordered-like. Developmental stages refer to the learning of several syntactic features (e.g. word order, negation, question formation). Language learners, no matter their first language, seem to follow a specific sequence in the learning of particular structures. They tend to access (output processing) information in stage 1 before stage 2, for example. The sample below (Table 2.1) refers to the stages learners would go through when learning and using 'negation' in English.

Another example is the acquisition of *ser* and *estar* (copular form of be) in Spanish (Table 2.2). Learners traverse particular stages in the acquisition of these structures (see table below on the acquisition of *ser* and *estar*).

Language learners must acquire stages 1 and 2, before the other stages. They can't skip stages, and language instruction can't be provided for learners to do something if they are not ready for learning.

The order of learning instead refers to the fact that language learners follow a particular order in the learning of language morphemes. What is a morpheme? A morpheme is a very small unit of language that carries a meaning. For example, the word *house* is a morpheme, and when we need to

**Table 2.1** Sequence of acquisition of negation in English

| Stage | Description | Example |
|---|---|---|
| 1 | At this stage, language learners can only make use of the negative word 'No' which appears before verbs or nouns. | *No drink*<br>*No speak* |
| 2 | At stage 2, language learners are able to use 'No' after the subject of the sentence. | *I no drink*<br>*I no speak* |
| 3 | At stage 3, the modal verb appears and the negation is attached to the verb. | *I can't drink*<br>*I can't speak* |
| 4 | At stage 4, 'do' appears and the negation is attached to the verb. | *I don't drink*<br>*I don't speak* |

**Table 2.2** Sequence of acquisition of *ser* and *estar* in Spanish

| Stage | Description |
|---|---|
| Stage 1 | Omission of copulas |
| Stage 2 | Use of *ser* for most communicative functions requiring a copula |
| Stage 3 | Discriminate use of *ser* to tell time |
| Stage 4 | Correctly replacing *ser* with *estar* for locating entities |
| Stage 5 | Correctly replacing *ser* with *estar* for forming progressive |
| Stage 6 | Discriminate use of *ser* for describing a referent's natural or inherent qualities |
| Stage 7 | Discriminate use of *ser* for stating origin |
| Stage 8 | Discriminate use of *ser* for identifying a subject or describing a referent's affiliation |
| Stage 9 | Discriminate use of *ser* for describing a referent's physical make-up |
| Stage 10 | Use of *estar* for conditions and resultant states |
| Stage 11 | Use of *estar* for describing a change from the norm |

refer to 'more than one' we add an -s- to this word. In this case, we have two morphemes, the root word *house* and the plural (more than one) marker -s-.

> **In a Nutshell ...**
>
> Language learning is constrained by orders, sequences and stages.

When it comes to verb morphemes, it has been proved that language learners would follow a specific learning order. For example, in English, language learners would learn the *-ing* morpheme (referring to a continuous action in the present) as in *playing* before the morpheme *-ed* (referring to a past action). The reason for this is that the morpheme *-ing* has, what we call, a higher communicative value than the morpheme *-ed*. This means that in a sentence such as *I am playing tennis* there are no other elements in the sentence except for *-ing* that carry the same meaning (the idea that the action is not completed in the present). On the contrary, the *-ed* morpheme is often made redundant by the presence of another element in the sentence (*Yesterday John called Anna*) encoding the same meaning (*Yesterday*), and this presence causes some delay in making a connection between a form and its meaning (*-ed* = express the meaning that an action has already taken place).

The sequence below illustrates the order of learning of some verb morphemes in English:

1. progressive *-ing*
2. regular past tense *-ed*
3. irregular past tense
4. third-person singular *–s*

The order and stage characteristics of language learning demonstrate that language learners have internal implicit mechanisms that process and organize language over time systematically and naturally.

> ### Reflect on This ...
> Can you provide an example of order and stages in language learning for another language?
>
> Knowing what we know about order and stages of language learning, what are the implications for the language classroom? Name a couple of implications:
>
> - 
> -

> **Reflect on This ...**
>
> Knowing what we know about order and stages of acquisition, what are the implications for language pedagogy?

# The Centrality of Implicit Learning

Learning language explicitly refers to the fact that we are conscious and intentional about what we are learning. For example, we can learn that in English to use a noun such as *car* in its plural form we must add an -s- to the noun such as in *cars*. In other words, we are aware of this 'rule' and we can consciously apply it to express the idea of 'more than one' (plurality) when necessary.

Implicit learning instead refers to the fact that we are unconscious about what we are learning and we can't verbalize any 'rules' of the language we are learning. However, we would be able to understand or use (not intentionally and implicitly) *cars* and not *car* in contexts that require us to refer to the concept of 'more than one'. We must then conclude that there is a qualitative difference between explicit and implicit learning (intentional vs. unintentional, conscious vs. unconscious, can be verbalized vs. can't be verbalized).

> **In a Nutshell ...**
>
> Language learning is fundamentally implicit.

One of the main fact that we know from L2 learning theory and research is that explicit learning does not turn into implicit learning. What does this finding mean for language teaching in the classroom?

In traditional language teaching, teachers provide language learners with long explanations about the grammatical rules of the language they are learning. Learners practise these rules mostly through a mechanical type of practice called 'drill'. At the end of the class, language teachers assess learners using language tests where they need to display their explicit knowledge about the forms practised.

There are *two main problems* with this type of classroom teaching aiming at developing explicit learning/knowledge: (1) it does not correspond to the way language develops in our mind; (2) it does not correspond to the way language learners process information. Chapter 6 provides a more detailed discussion about these matters.

Developing explicit knowledge is the ability to consciously process language to find out whether the language contains regularities and, if so, to work out the concepts and rules with which these regularities can be captured. However, language learning is implicit in nature and involves the unconscious processing of language. The role and nature of language and language processing are further discussed in Chapter 4 of this textbook.

## Quiz

Take the following short quiz to see what you have learned so far.

1. Learners' language system is …
   a. implicit
   b. explicit
   c. easy to describe

2. The main ingredient for the development of language is …
   a. Explicit information
   b. Input
   c. Output

3. The part of the input that has been attended to and processed is called …
   a. Language system
   b. Output
   c. Intake

4. What is the best example to describe good classroom input?
   a. The language teacher tells the learner what she did at the weekend in the target language
   b. Language teacher provides explicit information for the use of past tense
   c. Language teacher asks the learner to read the rules about the past tense in their textbook

5. When they attempt to make sense of the input they receive, language learners should …

   a. Skip over the meaning
   b. Skip over the form
   c. Make form-meaning connections

6. The development of the language system is …

   a. Ordered-like
   b. Explicit
   c. Frequency driven

7. Proponents of the view that language is implicit and abstract believe that …

   a. Humans are genetically equipped to learn a language
   b. Language learning depends on the frequency of the input
   c. Language learning involves recognizing patterns in the input

# Explicit Knowledge Does Not Turn into Implicit Knowledge

As previously highlighted, explicit and implicit learning are intrinsically different and one does not turn into another. The main view is that language learning is implicit. Language learning involves the development of what we call competence. Competence refers to the implicit and abstract knowledge of the language, similar to the one possessed by native speakers of their first language. We say implicitly because speakers generally are unaware of this knowledge, and even if aware

> **In a Nutshell …**
>
> Competence refers to the implicit and abstract knowledge of a language.

> **In a Nutshell …**
>
> - Explicit knowledge is conscious and explicit.
> - Implicit knowledge is unconscious and implicit.
> - Explicit does not turn into implicit.

they cannot articulate its contents. We say abstract because it does not consist of rules. Competence is not a list or set of rules and grammatical forms but instead a variety of abstract principles that interact to make sentences look the way they look to us. Competence is often contrasted with *performance*. Performance is something different and it refers to how humans use language in real situations.

The language system grows as our competence in the language grows. From this perspective, language development is the result of the interaction between input data and universal principles about the language humans possess. This interaction happens outside of learners' awareness. One of the key claims of this theory is that language is a complex and abstract system that develops in the human mind, and all humans possess an innate knowledge that regulates the learning of languages (see Chapter 4).

Language learning is also largely implicit and it is the result of the unconscious processing of linguistic data in the input. Language learning is a dynamic and evolving process in which several elements operate and are responsible for the emergence of the language system. Explicit processes do not result in the development of this implicit system.

---

### Reflect on This ...

If L2 learning is largely implicit, what are the main implications for language teaching in the classroom?

- 
- 
- 

Please read the following paper: VanPatten, B. (2016). Why explicit knowledge cannot become implicit knowledge. *Foreign Language Annals*, 49, 650–7.

---

An alternative position exists and suggests that language learning involves both implicit and explicit knowledge. Taking this view, L2 learning would entail going from the controlled mode of operation (declarative knowledge) to an automatic mode (procedural knowledge) through repeated practice. Declarative knowledge involves the learning of isolated facts and rules (e.g. *knowing that a car can be driven*).

Procedural knowledge requires practice and involves the processing of longer units and increasing automatization (e.g. *knowing how to drive a car*). This theoretical perspective addresses issues related to the way people develop fluency and accuracy. The view is that language learners need to be taught explicitly and need to practise the various grammatical features and skills (develop accuracy) until they are well established (fluency). According to this view, both explicit and implicit processes are at work. This view is that learners must notice language features in the input and need some kind of conscious awareness to acquire those features. One thing we should say here is that skill should be juxtaposed with the concept of competence. Skill refers to the ability to perform, and learning a skill is generally conceptualized as speaking, listening, reading and writing. Skill entails the interaction of two features: accuracy and fluency. Accuracy refers to the ability to do something correctly while fluency refers to the speed with which a person can do something. Competence is not a skill and can't be equated to fluency and accuracy. It refers to what learners have in their heads about language: the unconscious, implicit and generally abstract knowledge of the language.

> ## Reflect on This ...
> We have stated that explicit and implicit knowledge are qualitatively different. What does it mean for something to be qualitatively different from something else? Please explain.

Implicit learning is unconscious and involves the development of implicit and incidental knowledge (we do not know what it is, we do not know when we learned it and how we learned it). On the contrary, explicit learning is intentional. It happens, for example, when we are asked to repeat, utilize or memorize a grammar rule in the language classroom. Implicit learning is often linked to changes in learners' brain (see what the research is telling us in Table 2.2).

## What Neurolinguistic Research Is Telling Us about Implicit and Explicit Learning ...

- Implicit language learning is often linked to changes in the brain occurring in L2 learners after 'immersion language programmes' as opposed to 'college-based language programmes'.
- The superiority of immersion-based programmes does not lie in the fact that language learners abroad are more diligent not that they engage in more conversations. Their whole implicit learning system is way more stimulated abroad.
- All language is learned through memory (storage, consolidation, retrieval). Humans have different kinds of memory for 'notions' and 'sequences'. We have two long-term memory systems: one for notions (declarative memory system) and another for sequences (procedural memory system).
- Declarative knowledge cannot turn into procedural knowledge! Notions can be automatized and fastened up, but they cannot be turned into procedures.
- The brain needs time to process and learn information so we should prioritize comprehension over production.
- Exposure to unstructured, meaningful input-flood is essential!

## Takeaways from the Explicit and Implicit Knowledge Views

- Language learning is implicit in nature as it involves implicit learning.
- Language learning is implicit in nature and is the result of an interaction between universal/innate principles and input data.
- Competence is implicit (we are not aware of the knowledge and we can't articulate it) and abstract (there are no rules like the ones we find in textbooks but language formulas).
- Performance refers to how people use language in concrete situations.
- Skill is different from the concept of competence and it entails the interaction of two features: accuracy and fluency.

# What Is the Nature and Role of Output in Language Learning?

Output is the language that language learners produce in various contexts and carries some meaning. Is the language that learners produce through mechanical exercises in the classroom the kind of output necessary for L2 learning?

> **In a Nutshell ...**
>
> Output refers to the language that learners produce during communicative interactions to express meaning.

First of all, language learners must produce output for a communicative purpose as our definition of output refers to meaningful language that learners produce in various contexts and has a communicative purpose. The concept of output in language learning is linked to the concept of language production by the learner for a specific aim such as making a grocery list, planning a holiday, attending an interview or talking about our education and experience, among other things. Through language production (oral and written) language learners generate new knowledge and consolidate or modify their existing knowledge. Likewise, for input, the output must be language that has a specific meaning.

A distinction is often made between comprehensible output and modified output. Comprehensible output is the language produced by a speaker that is understandable by another interlocutor. Modified output, instead, refers to output that has been modified to ensure that another interlocutor understands it.

> **In a Nutshell ...**
>
> Output has a dual function:
> - to help the learner notice gaps in his speech production;
> - to help the learner check understanding of the speech production.

What does it mean? It means that meaningful output might have some facilitative roles in language learning: (1) it might help learners to notice new language (output provides input for someone else); (2) it might help learners to test hypotheses they have about the language. If the hypothesis 'works', then they will be inclined to continue using it. If it doesn't, then they will be more inclined to abandon it and search for a better hypothesis; (3) it might enhance the ability to negotiate meaning; (4) it might help the development of how language learners can connect sentences (discourse).

> **In a Nutshell ...**
>
> 'Negotiation' refers to the efforts, requests for clarification or confirmation that native and non-native speakers make to understand each other and make themselves understood during their interactions.

Meaningful output could help L2 learners verify their knowledge through oral or written production of the language. If their production 'works', then they will be inclined to keep talking or writing the same way. If not, they will be more inclined to look for a better and more correct way to express themselves.

Meaningful output can improve the ability to interact, negotiate the meaning of the interaction and help the learner to use the language through oral and written production. Production serves as a trigger to help the learner pay attention to the means of expression needed to communicate (we will discuss this important concept in Chapter 4). The output in the form of interaction with other interlocutors could have beneficial effects on language learning. The structure of the interaction between speakers can be modified and these modifications, called 'negotiations', can facilitate learning. 'Negotiation' refers to the efforts – and requests for clarification or confirmation – which native and non-native speakers make to understand each other and make themselves understood during their interactions. These discursive strategies provide learners with better-quality input. Input changes occur when one learner adjusts his or her speech due to perceived difficulties in understanding the other. The other learner may also indicate in some way that he hasn't understood. In terms of negotiation, the tools most commonly available and used by learners are the following:

- Clarification expressions can be defined as a way to clarify the meaning of a sentence that is not understood (e.g. What did you say?);
- Confirmatory expressions are used by learners and teachers when it is not 100 per cent clear what has been said (e.g. Did I understand correctly ...?);
- Expressions of understanding are used when a learner or a teacher is not convinced that the other has understood what has been said (e.g. Did you understand what I meant?).

Interaction can be defined as a situation where there is some kind of communicative exchange between the learner and at least one other learner or language teacher. Through these exchanges, learners have the advantage of being able to negotiate meaning and make some conversational adjustments to understand the language. For example, learners sometimes ask for clarification if they don't understand the meaning of the language they are exposed to. These types of expressions to foster interaction and understanding can have positive effects on language learning. Language learners must be exposed to understandable input and have the opportunity to interpret, communicate and negotiate the language through interaction.

> ### Reflect on This ...
>
> A reasonable conclusion to this chapter would state that comprehensible and meaningful input is necessary for language learning and the door remains open that communicatively embedded output may play an indirect role in language learning. Yet many people, including teachers, believe that you have to speak to 'learn the grammar' or 'learn the language'.
>
> Where do you think this belief comes from?
>
> Please read the following article: Lichtman, K., & VanPatten, B. (2021). Was Krashen right? Forty years later, *Foreign Language Annals*, 54, 283–305.

In testing hypotheses about language through its use, learners can develop fluency and automaticity through speech production. Little effort is required to perform an automatic process, involved when the student speaks or writes without awareness, as his task has become routine and automated just like in the development of any skill. We must bear in mind that the ability to produce shapes and textures through our output does not necessarily mean that these shapes and textures have been acquired. A distinction must be made between output as interaction with others and output as the practice of forms and structures. Implicit, as opposed to explicit, learners' systems develop as they understand the input they receive.

The role of output in L2 learning is important as it promotes our linguistic awareness and facilitates interaction with other interlocutors, but it does not play a direct role in creating the learner's language system. There is no experimental data which clearly demonstrate that learning is in any way dependent on output. We must also remember that there is a clear distinction between learning language skills and building up an implicit system. The explicit presentation of language rules and mechanical language production perhaps facilitates the development of certain skills to use certain forms/structures correctly and accurately in highly controlled linguistic situations and for a short period of time, but this has no impact on the development of the implicit system primarily responsible for learning of languages.

Input is not enough for developing the ability to use language in communicative context. Learners require access to the language system to string elements together in a sentence. Access can be defined as the ability for language learners (1) to express a particular meaning by retrieving a particular form or structure in the system and (2) to string structures and forms together. The fact that learners incorporate structures and forms in the language system does not mean they can have automatic access to them for speech production. The role and nature of interaction and feedback during language production are further discussed, respectively, in Chapters 6 and 8.

### What the Research Is Telling Us …

- While we accept that input is indispensable for language learning, output has a facilitative role.
- Interactions can facilitate the acquisition of lexical items (words) and their meanings and can promote the learning of some linguistic elements such as certain inflections of verbs and nouns.
- Interactions can be linked to skill development (speaking) and vocabulary development. However, they cannot be related to the development of competence seen as an implicit and mental representation of language.

## Reflect on This ...

Output is the language that learners produce and carries some kind of meaning.

Is mechanical practice such as drill practice the kind of output necessary for language learning?

Does output produced through drills have a communicative purpose?

## Takeaways from This Chapter

- Language learning is largely implicit.
- Explicit learning and implicit learning are different.
- Language learning is affected by natural orders (morphemes) and sequences (syntax).
- Competence and performance (skill) are two different concepts.
- Output plays a different role than input in language learning.
- Interaction can have a facilitative role in language learning.

# Knowing More about the Subject

Long, M. (2007). *Problems in SLA*. Erlbaum.

Paradis, M. (2009). *Declarative and procedural determinants of second languages*. John Benjamins.

Pienneman M., & Kessler, J.(2011). *Studying processability theory*. John Benjamins.

VanPatten, B. (2003). *From input to output*. McGraw-Hill.

VanPatten, B. (2010). Two faces of SLA: Mental representation and skill. *Journal of English Studies*, 10, 1–18.

VanPatten, B. (2016). Why explicit knowledge cannot turn into implicit knowledge. *Foreign Language Annals,* 49, 650–7.

VanPatten, B., & Smith, M. (2022). *Explicit and implicit learning.* Cambridge University Press.

# Further Clarifications

In this section, we aim to further clarify some of the terms or concepts presented in the chapter.

**Communicative value** refers to the level of meaning encoded by a form. For example, *-ing-* had a higher communicative value than *-s-* third-person singular in English. This is because in the case of *-ing-* there are no other elements in the sentence *I am playing chess* encoding the same meaning. In the case of the sentence *John plays chess* the third-person *-s-* is expressing the same semantic information (the idea that a third person does the action) is already encoded by the subject of the sentence (*John*).

**Competence** is used in this chapter to refer to the abstract and implicit nature of language possessed by native speakers. Abstract because we can articulate the content and it does not consist of rules as described in the textbook. Implicit because learners are not aware of having this knowledge. In the chapter the word performance is also used not expressing the same meaning. Performance cannot be equated to competence as it is how learners can use language in specific contexts and situations.

**Interaction** refers to conversations between learners and others and focuses on how such interactions might affect language learning.

**Noticing** is a concept used in second language learning theory to describe that there might be some level of awareness in learning a language. Language learners might have to notice linguistic elements in the input for those to be learned.

**Output** refers to the language that learners produce during communicative interactions or for the purpose of expressing a message.

**Output Processing** refers to the processing procedures used by learners to access the language system to be able to string together elements in a sentence.

**The mental representation of Language** is used in the chapter as a synonym for Competence. Mental representation is the abstract, complex and implicit language system which resides in the learner's mind. It is the underlying knowledge in our language system. It is opposed to the concept of skill which is merely the ability to use language in real time.

# 3
# What Are the Effects of Instructional Efforts in Language Learning?

> Overview 41
> What Is the Role of Instruction in Language Learning? 41
>   A Limited Role 43
>   A Facilitative Role 43
>   Motivation Has a Limited Role in Language Learning 47
> What Are the Main Implications for the Language Classroom? 48
> Knowing More about the Subject 52

## Overview

Researchers have investigated the role of instruction in second language learning. Instruction has a limited but beneficial role at least in speeding up language learning. In this chapter, you will explore two main questions (Figure 3.1): (1) What is the role of instruction in language learning?, (2) What are the main implications for the language classroom?

## What Is the Role of Instruction in Language Learning?

This is a central question in second language learning. Does language instruction make a difference? Very often the misleading answer to this

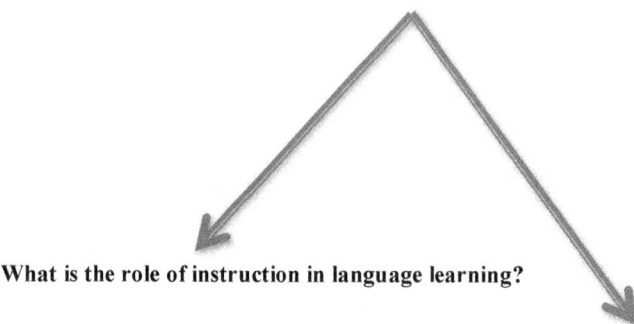

What is the role of instruction in language learning?

What are the main implications for the language classroom?

**Figure 3.1** Key questions of Chapter 3.

> **In a Nutshell ...**
>
> Instruction has a limited role in language learning, but it could facilitate the rate of learning.

question is that it does. The truth of the matter is that instruction has a very limited role.

Research on role of instruction in language learning has investigated its effects on the route (learning of various features in a specific order); the rate (learning of features at a specific speed) and the ultimate level of L2 attainment (reaching higher or lower of proficiency levels).

There are two main views on the role of language instruction in language learning:

1. Language instruction has a limited role;
2. Language instruction could have a beneficial role under certain conditions. The first condition is that it might bring learners' attention to things in the input that might not be appropriately processed (e.g. making correct form/word-meaning connections). Secondly, the language classroom can provide language learners with exposure to comprehensible and meaningful input. Language instruction might

> **In a Nutshell ...**
>
> A form-function connection refers to the grammatical function that a form plays in sentence interpretation or sentence meaning.

have a beneficial role in the rate (how quickly we can learn certain language elements) of learning.

## A Limited Role

Language instruction plays a limited role essentially because learning involves mainly unconscious and implicit processes. Comprehensible and message-oriented input are the two main ingredients for successful learning. Grammar is not learned through exposure to grammatical rules. Linguistic features are acquired in a specific order and sequence. In English progressive form *-ing* is acquired before regular past tense form-*ed*, which is acquired before third-person singular form *-s*. Language instruction is not able to alter the route of language learning. In terms of stages of learning such as in the case of the previous example on 'negation', language instruction can only be effective if it is targeted at features for which language learners are developmentally read. In this case, language instruction can be beneficial in helping learners to move faster along their natural route of development.

## A Facilitative Role

Language instruction might help learners to speed up learning particularly if opportunities for natural exposure are given. It might have a facilitative role if it facilitates the noticing of a form and subsequently the accurate processing of that form. Learners make form-meaning connections from the input they receive as they connect particular meanings to particular forms. Language instruction can have a facilitative role in helping language learners to process input more effectively (see Chapter 8 in this textbook for more information about this topic). Manipulating input might help learners to make necessary form-meaning connections. Language teachers should consider drawing learners' attention to properties of the language by exposing them to input-oriented and meaningful language.

Language instruction might, in certain conditions, speed up the rate of learning. What are the conditions that might facilitate the speed at which languages are learned?

- The first condition is that learners must be exposed to sufficient comprehensible and meaningful input.

- A second condition is that learners must be developmentally ready (ready to move from one stage to another as in the example of 'negation') for language instruction to be effective.
- A third condition is that language instruction must take into consideration how learners process input. Some elements of the language might be more or less difficult to process (*-ing* easier to process than *-s-* third-person singular in English, for example) and language instruction might have a role in facilitating processing.

Language instruction might be beneficial if it does circumvent underlying natural language processes.

### Reflect on This ...

Why is the morpheme *-ing-* easier to process than *-s-* third-person singular in English?

Can you provide another example in a different language?

Considering that language is complex, abstract and implicit, language instruction should not consist of an explanation of rules and mechanical practice. Traditional language instruction might help to develop a language-like behaviour (skill), but it is not responsible for language learning as a mental representation of language. Instead language instruction should be input-oriented and meaningful. A focus on form is a way to draw learners' attention to a form in a meaningful context (see Chapter 8 in the textbook for the development of pre-planned activities to focus on form such as textual enhancement and structured input activities.

### What the Research Is Telling Us ...

A basic review of the empirical evidence of studies investigating the role of language instruction in L2 learning suggests:

- Language instruction might help learners to develop a good level of attainment particularly if opportunities for natural exposure to language input are given.
- Language instruction has a facilitative role when it is used for linguistic features, which are not too distant from the learner's current level of language development.
- Language instruction might have a facilitative role in helping learners to pay selective attention to form and form-meaning connections in the input. Learners make form-meaning connections from the input they receive as they connect particular meanings to particular forms (grammatical or lexical).
- Language instruction should move from input to output practice. Initially, input-based and interactional options for instruction might help learners to internalize the grammatical features of a target language (see Chapter 8).

Overall, the role of language instruction in language learning is limited and constrained by several factors (e.g. orders and sequences of development, processing constraints). Despite that, it might have some beneficial effects in terms of speeding up the rate of language learning. The question is how. If we are going to focus on form in any way in the language classroom, it ought to be an input-based and meaning-oriented type of focus on form (see Chapter 8 for examples of how we can achieve this). Language instruction as input manipulation might facilitate language processing.

Language instruction should be less about the teaching of rules and more about exposure to form. Input (comprehensible and meaningful) is an indispensable element in language development. Instruction should make use of particular types of input manipulations (e.g. structured input) so that language learners make correct form-meaning connections.

Instruction ought to be less about manipulating output and more about processing input (input manipulations through input enhancement and structured input; see Chapter 8 in this textbook). Although output is constrained by processability stages, meaningful output practice (see Chapters 7 and 8 in this textbook) has a role in language learning. We also need to keep in mind that incidental learning is possible and desirable. One of the main conditions is that language learners would need to be exposed to input where they focus their attention on linguistic forms and their meaning through meaning-based activities.

## Reflect on This ...

If language instruction has a limited role, what is the role of grammar teaching in the language classroom? Identify three possible benefits.

- 
- 
- 

## Reflect on This ...

Is input necessary in language learning? Is input sufficient for L2 learning?

How do we make input more comprehensible and message oriented in language pedagogy? Provide few examples.

- 
- 
- 

**Quiz:** Take the following short quiz to see what you have learned since the last quiz. You can circle more than one option.

1. Order of acquisition refers to ...
   a. How learners acquire a particular form
   b. How learners produce a particular form
   c. How leaners interpret input easy to describe

2. A major benefit of instruction is...
   a. Teaching rules
   b. Expose learners to communicative input
   c. Repeating patterns of language

3. Stages of acquisition of particular features are...
   a. Common to all learners
   b. Can be skipped
   c. Apply only to certain languages

4. Learners normally process…
   a. All the input they hear
   b. Input based on processing strategies
   c. Only specific morphemes

## What the Research Is Telling Us about Second Language Learning …

- Language is implicit, complex and abstract in nature.
- Language learning is input-dependent. Learners require comprehensible and meaningful input to build their new language system.
- Language learning is processing dependent. Learners need to make accurate and appropriate form-meaning connections.
- Language learning is implicit. L2 learning involves the development of an implicit, abstract and complex language system.
- Language learning is constrained by orders and sequences.
- Language learning requires opportunities for meaningful interactions and output.

**Task:** Read Benati, A. (2014). Second language acquisition. In C. Fäcke (ed.), *Language acquisition* (pp. 179–97). New York: Mouton de Gruyter; identify the main givens in relation to learning another language.

- 
- 
- 
- 

# Motivation Has a Limited Role in Language Learning

Motivation in language learning refers to language learners' willingness to learn. There is a belief that motivation is a strong predictor of successful

> **In a Nutshell …**
>
> Motivation does not affect the underlying processes and mechanisms involved in language learning.

L2 learning. The assumption is that because motivation is a key factor in learning many skills in life, it should also influence the learning of a language. It is believed by many that the more motivated we are, the more there is a chance for learning a language. However, we should consider two factors before jumping to such a conclusion: (1) learning a second language is not like learning any other skills; language is not a skill (see also Chapter 2). Motivation is not able to explain the complex mechanisms involved in L2 learning. While research on motivation can partially explain why some learners might acquire more of the second language compared to other learners, this research has failed to explain both how language gets into our minds, and what language gets into our minds. Motivation does not affect the underlying processes and mechanisms involved in L2 learning no matter how much an individual is motivated. It does not affect ordered development or the role of universals in L2 learning, for example.

# What Are the Main Implications for the Language Classroom?

Drawing from theory and research in L2 learning we can highlight some key principles to keep in mind if we intend to develop effective language pedagogy for the classroom:

- Language teachers should provide learners with meaningful and comprehensible input.
- Language teachers should prioritize incidental and implicit learning.
- Language teachers should provide learners with level-appropriate input and interaction.
- Language teachers should provide learners with a focus on grammar that is input-oriented and meaning-focused.
- Language teachers should engage learners with language which is produced to interpret and express meaning.
- Language teachers should provide learners with implicit corrective feedback and correction should be kept to a minimum.

- Language teachers should move from input to output practice following the learning model proposed.

Below are some of the frequently asked questions from language teachers to improve language classroom pedagogy.

> **Frequently Asked Questions from Language Teachers**
>
> *Do language learners acquire language via comprehensible and meaningful input?* YES
> Comprehensible input remains the foundation of all language learning. Language learning is input-dependent, and learners must be engaged in language comprehension to construct that system (see Chapter 6).
>
> *Can we change the natural order of language learning?* NO
> Acquiring a language is constrained by particular orders and stages. Language features such as morphemes are processed by learners following particular orders.
>
> *Does explicit knowledge turn into implicit knowledge?* NO
> What we call grammar rules are what we have in our minds. Acquisition of a language system is input-dependent, and language is complex, abstract and implicit (see Chapter 4).
>
> *Is the 'Question and Answer' type of practice the same as communication?* NO
> Language learning is the interaction between communicatively embedded language that learners hear or see, innate universal mechanisms about language, and processing mechanisms that mediate between input and the internal language system. Communication is not simply speaking or answering questions. Communication is the interpretation, expression and negotiation of meaning in a specific context and for a specific purpose (see Chapter 7).
>
> *Should we teach and practice specific grammar points explicitly?* NO
> No meaningful support has been provided for the position that grammar should be explicitly taught. Things like person-number endings on verbs must be learned from the input like anything else

as they can't be taught and practised to build the language system. The input approach to grammar instruction works about six times as quickly as traditional teaching (see Chapter 8). A focus on grammar should be input-oriented and meaning-based. Traditional instruction only helps to develop 'a language-like behaviour'.

### Does corrective feedback improve language learners' competence? NO

While language teachers like recasting (and do it a lot), and while learners can and do immediately generate improved output as a result, these interactions are not associated with improved competence (see Chapters 8 and 9). Neither explicit information nor explicit feedback seems to be crucial for a change in performance.

### Does vocabulary memorization and choral repletion help? NO

Words are learned in context. The main bulk of vocabulary happens through comprehension. Learners process content words first. Vocabulary leads to the acquisition of grammar as words have meaning and grammatical properties (see Chapter 5).

Task: Read Wong, W., & VanPatten, B. (2004). Beyond experience and belief. *Foreign Language Annals*, *37*(1), 133–42. Identify the main arguments for the non-necessity of drills in language teaching!

- 
- 
- 

## Task: Applying the Knowledge and Information

The main purpose of this task is to summarize four main findings in L2 learning theory and research and do the following:

- Explain how these findings undermine existing and 'popular beliefs' for language learning and teaching.
- Identify possible and practical implications for language teaching in a specific target language.

| Research findings | Popular beliefs | Implications for teaching |
|---|---|---|
|  |  |  |

## Takeaways Some Basic Principles in Contemporary Language Teaching!

- Adopt a clear definition of communication.
- Language should not be treated like a skill.
- Quality of input and opportunities for interaction are key elements.
- The use of interactive tasks is beneficial.
- A 'focus on form' in the input should be meaningful.

## Takeaways from This Chapter

- Instruction has a limited but facilitative role in language learning.
- Language is not a skill.
- There are several implications from language learning theory and research useful for language teaching (see above list of basic principles).

## Knowing More about the Subject

Benati, A. (2020). *Key questions in language teaching.* Cambridge University Press.
Benati, A. (2022). *Key terms for language teachers.* Equinox.
Hinkel, E. (ed.) (2005). *Handbook of research in second language teaching and Learning.* Lawrence Erlbaum Associates.
Long, M. H. (2015). *Second language acquisition and task-based language teaching.* Routledge.
Lowen, S. (2020). *Introduction to second language acquisition.* Routledge.
Malovrh, P. A., & Benati, A. G. (eds) (2019). *The handbook of advanced proficiency in second language acquisition.* Wiley Blackwell.
VanPatten, B., & Rothman, J. (2014). Against 'rules'. In A. Benati, C. Laval & M. J. Arche (eds), *The grammar dimension in instructed second language acquisition: Theory, research, and practice* (pp. 15–35). Bloomsbury.
VanPatten, B., & Benati, A. (2015). *Key terms in second language acquisition.* Bloomsbury.

## Further Clarifications

In this section, we aim to further clarify some of the terms or concepts presented in the chapter.

**Communication** is not about speaking or question and answer. Instead, it is the interpretation, expression and negotiation of meaning in a given context and for a specific purpose.

**Focus on form** is about drawing language learners' attention to certain linguistic features in the input they are exposed to.

**Language task** is a language-learning endeavour that requires students to (1) comprehend, (2) manipulate and (3) produce the target language as they perform some set of work plans. Tasks provide learners with a purpose for language use and make language teaching more communicative.

**Motivation** is a concept difficult to define in language learning. Generally it refers to the desire of the language learner to learn.

**Ultimate attainment** refers to a point at which learners seem to stop progressing. We say that their language system has reached stasis.

# 4

# What Is Language? And What Is the Relevance for the Language Classroom?

Overview 53
What Is the Nature and Role of Language? 54
  Abstract System 55
  Complex System 57
  Implicit System 58
  Language and Communication 61
  Language and Culture 62
What Are the Main Implications for the Language Classroom? 64
Knowing More about the Subject 67

## Overview

Language is a complex, abstract, implicit system, and the rules we know and usually learn from language textbooks are not the rules we have in our minds. What speakers have in their minds is an abstract system, and pedagogical rules describe only the surface parts of the language (sentences) but not the underlying information. This chapter discusses the nature and role of language and the pedagogical implications which arise for the language classroom (Figure 4.1).

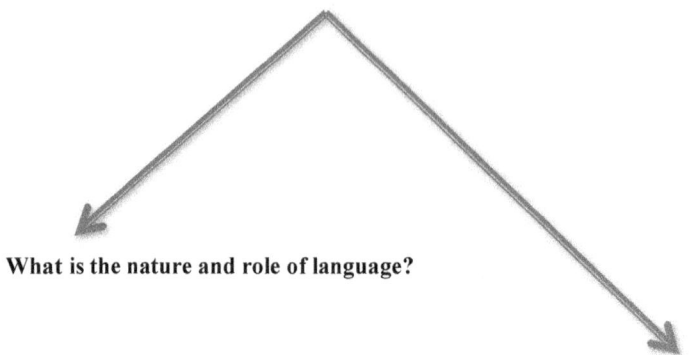

What is the nature and role of language?

What are the main implications for the language classroom?

**Figure 4.1** Key questions of Chapter 4.

# What Is the Nature and Role of Language?

Language teacher education programmes should aim at ensuring that teachers develop a good understanding of how principles derived from theory and research can be applied to language teaching. These programmes are often module-based covering a range of areas and issues including how to teach grammar or how to develop language skills through classroom practice. However, one of their limitations is that they don't include a module discussing the nature and role of language.

> ### Task: Can You Define Language?

Language teachers do not have an accurate understanding of what language is. Most often, they believe it is a set of rules, it represents a system for communication or it is learned through culture. None of these three beliefs is correct as they are not derived from a careful and scientific analysis of what language is. Lack of knowledge of the language and how it works often leads to misleading claims and the belief that the rules we find in textbooks represent what we call 'grammar'. A common assumption is that 'knowing a language' involves knowing the words of a language and knowing its 'rules'. The consequences of this definition are the use of traditional approaches to teaching such as the Grammar-Translation Method or the Audiolingual Method. Traditional approaches to language teaching have separated out the teaching of vocabulary and the teaching of grammar despite the fact that there is a good body of research to suggest that the words/rules separation isn't so separate. There are indeed 'rules', generalizations and patterns in language. However, the rules are not the starting place for language learning. It is clear that morphemes, for example, are acquired as parts of words and phrases, and not in isolation. For example, even if learners are given a 'third-person singular rule' for verbs, such an explicit rule is not internalized through 'practice'. Rather, it develops or emerges as a pattern expressing regularity and is used productively only after having generalized over similar items encountered in communicative samples of language (input).

Language is not a skill and is not learned in the same way we learn subjects such as history, literature or any other discipline. You also don't learn it by practice as you do in the case of other skills such as learning to play tennis, chess or drive a car. Language is an abstract, complex and implicit system. Let's see its characteristics one by one.

# Abstract System

What does it mean that language is an abstract system? The answer to this question is not easy since it is difficult to describe the language if we are not specialists. The basic constructs of the language are largely indefinable in everyday terms. For example, what is a verb? A verb in any language can represent a variety of concepts such as an action (*sprint*), a state (*hang on*) or an experience (*love*). However, what kind of verb is it *to snow*, for example? It's not an action, and does not match the other categories, so what is it? The concept of a verb is an abstract concept that defies any accurate description and definition we have attempted.

Another example concerns the use of determiners. In a language textbook, rules such as *my* and *theirs* in English are described as possessive adjectives. Although both indicate the concept of possessing something, they are not considered by linguists as adjectives. Linguists called them 'determinants'.

In the English language, two determiners are not allowed in a sentence like *the my car*. However, in Italian, in the same sentence, this is possible (*la mia macchina*) because *mia* is actually an adjective. The question then is: What is a determiner? Can we define it objectively?

The point is that, even if we all think we know what a verb is, we sometimes have difficulty describing its nature and its role in the language. We simply recognize one when we see one. Constructs such as verbs, adjectives, determiners and other linguistic elements are abstract concepts that defy any accurate description or definition. There are also aspects of the language that are considered innate, for example, what is allowed and what is not allowed in a language. For example, native English speakers know implicitly whether the linguistic contractions below are allowed or not:

1. I' am not tired (is allowed)
2. I' may not arrive (not allowed – *may not* cannot be contracted)

> **In a Nutshell ...**
>
> Constructs such as verbs, adjectives, determiners and other linguistic elements are abstract concepts.

How does a person know, without having received any kind of instruction, when this contraction is allowed or not? The answer is that the human brain has a genetically determined specialization that is aimed at language. We all have, from birth, internal structural principles that help us learn the language. This is because the data we are exposed to is not rich enough to capture every feature of the language.

> **Reflect on This ...**
>
> If someone asks us to describe what a verb is, what should we answer?

Language is an implicit system composed of a vast network of forms and lexical items. This network is a map of grammatical and lexical items linked to each other through connections demonstrating semantic (relation based on meaning such as between *thrilling* and *exciting*), lexical (root word relationship such as *move* and *moving*), and formal relationships (a relationship between on grammatical form that does not change the meaning of the root but when added produces a new word such as *interesting* and *interested*). The network grows in our heads as we process more language and make more connections. However, language as a mental representation does not consist of rules. What every human creates in the mind/brain is a complex, abstract and implicit representation of language. What we observe as language is the result of a complex interaction of principles, constraints and interfaces that yield sentences.

> **Reflect on This ...**
>
> What are the implications of this view that language is abstract for language teaching in the classroom?
>
> List at least three main implications:
>
> 1.
> 2.
> 3.

## Complex System

Language can be described as a multi-component and complex system. Learning a language means acquiring several elements at the same time. The set of words is called the lexicon. Learners acquire words when they can assign a meaning to each word (these are called form-meaning connections). The verb bought means that my action happened in the past. The word car refers to a four-wheeled vehicle. Also, there are some other properties by which that word has a specific role in

> **In a Nutshell ...**
>
> Each sentence is a complex and abstract interaction between lexicon, syntax, phonology and morphological elements.

a sentence. The word *car* describing a four-wheeled vehicle represents an object in the sentence. It is also marked by the fact that in the singular it can coexist with both *a* and *the* (*I bought a/the car*). Words are inserted into sentences, but they can't just be inserted anywhere. There is a complex interaction between their meanings (if any), their syntactic properties (word order in the sentence) and other components that determine their use.

Phonology is the sound that makes up words (pronunciation) and how they come together to form speech. The phonological representation of a plural marker in English is /s/. However, the sounds are not always /s/ as in this case; there may be other sounds such as /z/ or /iz/.

Morphology refers to patterns of word formation (e.g. inflections on verbs and nouns). *Car* and *cars* are different because one has a plural marker and the other doesn't. *Cars* with an *-s* at the end of the word mean more than one.

Syntax refers to the constraints of sentence structure to explain which word combination is allowed or not in a language. English, like many Romance languages, is a language with a Subject-Verb-Object (SVO) syntactic typology since normally the subject of the sentence must be at the beginning and the verb in the middle before the object of the sentence (*Gaia bought a car*). The opposite is the case of the Japanese language, for example, which is a language with a different structure and syntactic order Object-Subject-Verb (OSV), where the verb is always at the end of the sentence (*Gaia a car bought*).

Learning a language means acquiring all these elements simultaneously. Every person, no matter if it is a first, second, or third language, develops a mental language system that we call language. This system is complex and abstract in nature as its characteristics are difficult to describe exactly. What we observe as language is the result of a complex interaction of principles and constraints that interact with each other and with the data provided by language input.

## Implicit System

The language system is also implicit since we know we have language in our heads, but we don't know what its characteristics are. As previously described, this implicit system is a vast network of lexical forms and items. This web of form-meaning connections grows through multiple exposures to the language. Rules are not the key ingredient for language learning. Even if we provide explicit information about a rule (*-ed* past tense ending in English), that rule is not internalized through practise. It can only emerge regularly in our speech after language learners have been exposed to that word (*-ed* past tense ending in English) through message-oriented language input.

The important thing is to be able to understand the language and the meaning of its elements and to make appropriate form-meaning connections.

Language has an underlying hierarchical structure consisting of sentences: (1) noun phrase (NP), (2) verb phrase (VP) and (3) prepositional phrase (PP). Each of these phrases requires a 'main element' and a 'complement'. To be clear, the main element that determines the syntactic category of the sentence *Gaia teaches Italian at the university* is *Gaia*. The verb *teaches* is the main element of the verbal phrase. The main constituent of the prepositional phrase is 'at the university' because this is the constituent that expresses the prepositional sense of the phrase. A complement is an option that accompanies or qualifies various sentences. Sentences have a hierarchical structure made up of these two constituents: main element and complement.

- Noun Phrase (NP) = Noun (main element) + complement = *Gaia is a professor*
- Verb Phrase (VP) = Verb (main element) + complement = *teaches Italian*
- Prepositional Phrase (PP) = Preposition (main element) + complement = *at the University*

All the information contained in the above sentences interacts in our minds. Language learners do not need input to know that the language has a hierarchical system and consists of sentences. Such information is an implicit part of the universal properties and principles of languages which are shared across all languages and are innate to all human beings.

Language develops over time through consistent and constant exposure to input data interacting with this innate knowledge and principles. This innate knowledge needs input from a given language to know if there are any variations. For example, English is syntactically an SVO type (*Alexander destroyed the car*), while Japanese is an OSV type (*the car Alexander destroyed*). As mentioned in Chapter 1, such variations between languages are called linguistic parameters. For English learners to mentally construct an OSV system if they learn Japanese, they need to be exposed to the language to be able to mentally interact with the principles of the new language and reset its parameters from SVO to OSV syntactic order.

> ### Reflect on This ...
>
> English is an SVO language and Japanese an OSV language in terms of word order.
>
> What about other Romance languages such as French or Spanish?
>
> Can you provide an example?

Language as mental representation refers to the complex, abstract, underlying linguistic system in the mind of the learner. It is implied because we are unaware of it and cannot describe its contents in exact words. A rather different understanding and definition of language is the concept of language as a skill. As said in Chapter 1, language skill is the ability to use language in real-time and involves the intersection of accuracy and fluency. Accuracy refers to how well learners can produce sentences without making any mistakes. Fluency, on the other hand, refers to how well learners can use the language with a certain speed and confidence. However, fluency and accuracy do not explain or represent what language actually is.

> ### Reflect on This ...
>
> What are the implications in your view of the fact that language learners have to develop a mental representation of language which is implicit in nature?

> ### What the Research Is Telling Us ...
>
> - Fact 1: Language is an abstract, complex and implicit system that relates sound (or signs) and meaning.
> - Fact 2: Learners develop an internal and unconscious representation of language.

- Fact 3: Language acquisition involves linking meaning/function to linguistic forms in the input during comprehension and strengthening these links through language use (comprehension and production).

## Language and Communication

Although language is a system residing in our minds, it is also true that we use language to communicate. However, communication and language are not the same things. Language can be part of communication, but it is not equivalent to communication. Communication is the expression and interpretation

> **In a Nutshell ...**
>
> Communication is a behaviour that takes place between people and communities. Language is the mental representation of a system that is of an abstract, complex and implicit nature.

of meaning in a given context and for a specific purpose (see Chapter 5). Central to this definition is the construct of meaning. Meaning refers to the information contained in the message we intend to convey. If someone says, for example, 'it's cold,' the literal meaning of the sentence is that it is cold. However, the meaning of this sentence can also refer to an intent. Perhaps the interlocutor who says 'it's cold' is concerned that someone else is not wearing enough clothes and he/she will catch a cold. When we express meaning, there is always someone else who has to interpret our message.

Context influences the way we communicate. Context refers to the participants and the environment – in other words, the social context in which we find ourselves. These two constructs interact to prompt us how to communicate differently under different situations and conditions. When we communicate, we always have some reason to convey a specific message. We might want to be social with others, make friends, get a job done, find out something, inform someone about something and entertain someone or a group of people. However, while the context might change, the language doesn't change. Communication is a social act because it takes place between multiple entities in a particular context.

For example, we could say, 'See how communication and language are not the same things?' or we could say, 'By now you should have an idea of why communication and language are not the same things.' These are two stylistic choices based on how we want or not to invite people to think about something. From a language perspective, independently from the communicational one, the verb to be used must be *are* and not *is*, and it must appear in only one place in both sentences. This is because the language does not change depending on the purpose. Language is a mental system that we draw on when communicating, but it doesn't have the same characteristics as communication.

Many think that language and communication are the same things, but in reality, they are not. Language is the mental representation of a system that has the following characteristics: it is abstract, complex and implicit. It consists of a variety of components that interact to create even the simplest sentences. Communication is a behaviour that takes place between people and communities. It is shaped by the social context and manifests itself in different ways depending on who is communicating with whom and for what purpose. How we communicate can be inextricably linked to culture, whatever it is. But language as a mental representation is not.

## Language and Culture

We often hear that culture is important for language teaching. We would certainly agree that culture is important when we want to learn about other people or other ways of doing and living. However, the teaching of culture does not affect language learning. The idea that it is necessary to know the culture to learn the language or that it is necessary to learn the language through culture is inaccurate and misleading. First, culture is an elusive concept. Even though we can define and talk about language and communication here, we have difficulty finding an operational and accurate definition of the nature of culture. Culture can include everything from religious and cultural beliefs to rules about polite behaviour and to the value we place on pets. And even within a culture, there can be cultures and subcultures.

The Japanese language has a very precise syntactic structure and we can think of at least three cultures that, despite being distinct from each other and separated both by time and space, share the same syntactic order as Japanese among all three. The fact of the matter is that culture is not at all implicated in the development of the mental system we call language.

Communication makes use of language, and language is part of the tools people use to acquire cultural knowledge while interacting by communicating. Language teachers may choose to place a strong emphasis on the development of cultural knowledge, especially if it is relevant to student's interests or if there is some social, political or other need. But we caution against the position that the formal properties and principles of language are learned through culture.

## Takeaways ...

Three aspects at the heart of the nature of language:

- It is an abstract system.
- It is a complex system.
- It is an implicit system.

We have also distinguished between communication and language, showing that they are not the same thing. Communication is a social activity that can make use of language, but language is something that resides in our minds whether we communicate or not. Communication depends on the creation of meaning and the roles of context and purpose, while neither of these constructs affects the very nature of language. That is, if an English-speaking person is in a doctor's office one moment, in a grocery store an hour later and then at home with a spouse, the English in that person's head does not change because the context of the communication is changed. The subject of a sentence is the subject of a sentence regardless of meaning, context and purpose. We also clarified the difference between language and culture and cautioned that the formal properties of language are not learned through culture.

**Quiz:** Take the following short quiz to see what you have learned in this chapter. You can circle more than one option.

1. Language as a mental system is ...

    a. Explicit
    b. Difficult to describe
    c. A set of rules

2. Language is…
   a. A skill
   b. Ability to perform
   c. Mental competence

3. Language and communication…
   a. Are different
   b. Language is part of communication
   c. Are basically the same

# What Are the Main Implications for the Language Classroom?

Language is a complex and special system and is not learned in the same way as other mental phenomena. What we observe as language is the result of a complex system that develops implicitly and unconsciously.

There is a belief among teachers and professionals that language is represented by the rules and explanations found in textbooks. Some of the old beliefs perpetuated by this view include that explicit teaching of grammar is necessary and that systematic practice of grammar rules aids learning. When we discussed the nature of language earlier, we argued that providing explicit information and giving rules does not facilitate its learning. Language is a complex, abstract and implicit system that exists in the learner's head.

Language is not the rules and explanations that appear on the pages of textbooks. What ends up in the human mind bears no resemblance to what we find on the pages of textbooks. Language teachers often explain the rules and this is followed by mechanical exercises called drills. Such a practice does very little to aid language development and only tends to forge behaviour very different from learning (see Chapter 6). The language to which learners are exposed in communicative contexts constitutes an effective system for facilitating language development (implicit knowledge) and providing good-quality input.

In traditional grammar-oriented instruction, one of the main assumptions is that language is learned through the inference of its properties. The teaching of grammar mainly consists of the study of forms and structures through the memorization and translation of texts. It is also suggested that grammar is learned through a process of repetition, imitation and reinforcement. Grammatical structures are presented linearly without any attention to meaning. These traditional approaches emphasize the use of memorization and pattern exercises as grammar teaching tasks and help develop 'language-like behaviour' in the language learner.

The so-called PPP (presentation-practice-production) proposes a three-stage model for language teaching. The first stage is the conscious and explicit learning of a grammatical form or structure. The second stage involves the systematic practice of this syntactic form or structure. In the final phase, activities involving the mechanical use of the target shape or structure are organized. The PPP suggests the use of activities that allows the student to move from a systematic use to an appropriate use of the language in the context. It is only when students have mastered the form that they will be able to use it in a context where the message becomes more important than the medium.

> ## Reflect on This ...
> 
> The traditional and mechanical approach involves several problems:
> 
> 1. It forces language learners to produce grammatical forms before they can understand the forms, which leads to incorrect generalizations and overuse of the form when it would not be necessary. Learners must have the opportunity to understand the language before being able to use it accurately.
> 2. It does not allow learners to make form-meaning connections level of understanding. The idea that grammar acquisition can be achieved simply by learning the grammatical rules of a target language and practising those rules through (most often mechanical and traditional) production has been challenged by many scholars in the field of language acquisition research.
> 3. It does not allow learners to learn those aspects of language which are individual to languages and can only be learned through exposure (lexical and morphological forms) to the language.
> 
> So how do we provide effective grammar teaching in the language classroom?

A traditional grammar-oriented approach is often characterized by long explicit explanations of specific linguistic forms or structures. The explicit explanation is followed by mechanical practice which consists of transformation and substitution exercises. In this type of so-called drill practice, real-life situations are completely ignored and the practice is implemented in a completely decontextualized way (see Chapter 6).

Bearing in mind the nature of the language, rather than teaching the language, we should try to create the necessary conditions to facilitate its learning. We must maximize opportunities for language learners to interpret and express meaning via targeted linguistic forms.

Input manipulation and pedagogical interventions facilitate the acquisition of lexical and morphological forms. Unlike traditional instruction, where the focus of teaching is on the explanations of rules and practice, input-based pedagogical interventions such as textual enhancement or structured input (see Chapter 6) aim to change the way the input is perceived by learners, foster form-meaning connections and facilitate language development. Input must be understandable, message-oriented and easy to process to affect language learning.

## What the Research Is Telling Us ...

- Language is an abstract and complex system and is not learned explicitly.
- Language can't be equated to grammatical rules that appear on the pages of manuals. Explicit rules cannot affect this abstract and complex system because the two are completely different. We learn words (starting point) which contain patterns.
- There is no internal mechanism capable of converting the explicit rules of textbooks into the implicit mental representation that is language.
- There are aspects of the language that cannot be learned (they are innate or derive from innate and universal principles).

## Takeaways from This Chapter

- Language is abstract, complex and implicit.
- Explicit teaching does not turn into implicit knowledge.

# Knowing More about the Subject

De Keyser, R. M. (1995). Learning second language grammar rules: An experiment with a miniature linguistic system. *Studies in Second Language Acquisition*, *17*, 397–410.

DeKeyser, R. M. (2020). Skill acquisition theory. In B. VanPatten, G. D. Keating & S. Wulff (eds), *Theories in second language acquisition* (pp. 83–104). Routledge.

Robinson, P., & Ellis, N. (eds) (2008). *Handbook of cognitive linguistics and second language acquisition*. Routledge.

Sharwood Smith, M., & Truscott, J. (2014). *The multilingual mind*. Cambridge University Press.

Ullman, M. (2020). The declarative-procedural model. In B. VanPatten, G. D. Keating & S. Wulff (eds), *Theories in second language acquisition* (pp. 128–61). Routledge.

VanPatten, B. (2018). *Communication and Skill*. Routledge.

VanPatten, B. (2018). *Language*. Routledge.

VanPatten, B. (2019). *The nature of language: A short guide to what's in our heads*. American Council on the Teaching of Foreign Languages.

VanPatten, B., & Benati, A. (2015). *Second language acquisition: Key terms*. Bloomsbury.

VanPatten, B., & Rothman, J. (2014). Against rules. In A. Benati, C. Laval & M. Arche (eds), *The grammar dimension in instructed second language learning* (pp. 15–35). Bloomsbury.

# Further Clarifications

In this section, we aim to further clarify some of the terms or concepts presented in the chapter.

**Explicit knowledge/learning** is used in this chapter to refer to knowledge or process related to conscious language learning. The learner is fully aware of learning as he/she can explain and articulate some of the concepts and linguistic features of the language.

**Implicit knowledge/learning** refers in this chapter to the abstract system and implicit processes related to language learning. The learner is not aware and cannot articulate any of the concepts and linguistic features of the language.

**Lexical/Lexicon refers** in this chapter to the mental dictionary we all carry around in our heads. Words in the mental lexicon are quite complex in that they carry more than just meaning.

**Morphemes/Morphology** refers in this chapter to how words are formed, that is, the pieces and parts of words and what they mean or what function they serve.

**Syntax** is referred to in this chapter as a component of language related to how sentences are implicitly formed (e.g. Subject-Verb-Object). Syntax refers to the universal properties and principles responsible for how language is processed and shaped up in our minds.

# 5

# Is There a More Dynamic Way to Organize the Language Classroom?

Overview  69

What Is the Role of Language Teachers and Learners in the Classroom?  70

How Do We Learn and Teach Vocabulary?  80

   Three Principles of Effective Vocabulary Teaching  84

Knowing More about the Subject  88

## Overview

In this section of the textbook, the new role played by language teachers and learners in the classroom will be examined. These are roles that must be conducive to communication, opportunities for interaction and effective in learning. The role and nature of vocabulary learning will also be examined and discussed. Vocabulary is not learned by repetition or learning words by heart. The chapter is organized around two main questions (Figure 5.1).

   Chapter 5
   Is there a more dynamic way to organize the language classroom?

# 70 Second Language Teacher Education

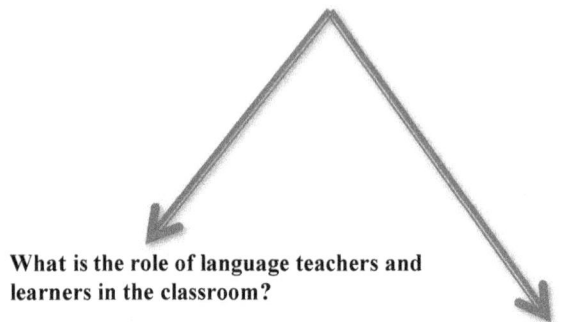

**Figure 5.1** Key questions of Chapter 5.

## What Is the Role of Language Teachers and Learners in the Classroom?

The role of language teachers and learners in the classroom has evolved over the years. In the very traditional method, the so-called *Grammar Translation Method*, the role of the language teachers was very authoritative and the language target was not the medium for instruction. This traditional methodology was a teacher-centred method of teaching, where learning consisted of being able to read and translate a text into and out of the target language.

In the *Audiolingual Method*, a method in vogue in the 1950s but still currently used, language teachers play the role of leaders and are responsible for providing learners with a good language model. Learners must imitate the model provided very much like parrots by following all the instructions and practices. They are exposed to correct models/patterns of the target language, and practice consists of a type of exercise called 'drill'. A drill is a practice where learners need to repeat, manipulate or transform a particular form or structure to complete the required exercise which is very mechanical.

When language learners are asked to engage in exercises that focus on specific grammatical properties of the language, rather than meaning, they normally follow a very structural syllabus. The main goal of this structural syllabus is for language learners to become accurate in the use of the target language. This view derives from an old language learning theory called

*Behaviourism* which argued that humans learn a language by imitating good habits. This is not the case, as learning languages is a more complex endeavour that involves cognitive and linguistic factors and not simply imitating a behaviour.

> **In a Nutshell ...**
>
> To foster language learning, language teachers should provide good comprehensible and meaningful input in the language classroom.

A more natural, communicative and effective approach to language teaching in the classroom is based on the need for the creation of a kind of environment that resembles the condition where L1 learning takes place. The assumption is that if language learners were exposed to 'comprehensible' input and were provided with opportunities to focus on the meaning and the message of that input rather than on grammatical forms and accuracy, they would be able to learn a second language in much the same way as they learn the first one.

To foster language learning, language teachers should provide good comprehensible meaningful input in the language classroom. Teachers should create a good classroom environment in which language learners are engaged in a wide range of meaning-based classroom activities.

> **In a Nutshell ...**
>
> New dynamic role for language teachers and learners where tasks dictate roles.

In the modern, dynamic and interactive language, classroom tasks must dictate the roles of both language teachers and learners. Both language teachers and learners must play specific roles. Language teachers must aim at providing learners with the opportunity to use the language in a natural, interactive and communicative context. Learners need to work to complete a specific task where they have plenty of opportunities for interaction, negotiation of meaning and use of language to express meaning.

The essential characteristics of a language task are the following: (1) meaning must play a key role, (2) learners must resolve a real problem and (3) learners are assessed in terms of the task outcome.

In a traditional approach to language teaching, the role of the language teacher is to teach the language and transfer his/her knowledge to the learner. The role of the learner is simply one of receiving passively that knowledge.

The example below illustrates the transmission role of the language teacher and the receptacle role of the language learner in the classroom.

Step 1. The teacher is giving language learners about fifteen minutes to complete individually a worksheet containing a multiple-choice activity (filling in the blanks with the correct grammatical element).

Step 2. At the end of the fifteen minutes, the teacher instructs language learners to work in small groups and check the answers.

Step 3. The teacher addresses the classroom and begins going over the correct answers one by one. The teacher reads each sentence in the classroom and calls on individual learners to respond. Language learners provide the correct element to complete the sentence.

Step 4. The teacher offers a lengthy explanation of particular grammatical elements both in the case when the learner gives a correct or incorrect answer.

> **In a Nutshell ...**
>
> - New roles for the teacher: support person and planner.
> - New roles for the learner: information finder and co-worker.

In the above example, all actions, interactions and explanations are dictated by the language teachers who play the role of the language expert. The language learner's main role is to receive that knowledge. The language teacher does not provide opportunities for the learner to use language in a meaningful and communicative way. The language learner's main role is to practise grammar by repeating and substituting new elements of the language into pre-planned structural and meaningless patterns, where the production of language is very restricted. In other words, language learners engaging in this type of practice would produce accurate sentences mechanically without knowing what they are saying. A traditional approach for the organization of the language classroom has long been the so-called PPP approach (presentation, practice, production). In this approach, individual language items are first presented by the language teacher and then practised in the form of spoken and written exercises called pattern drills.

In the modern language classroom, the role of the language teacher and the language learner has changed focusing on the need to develop authentic communication. The new role taken by both teachers and learners is based on the view that interaction between speakers is a multi-layered communicative event. Language learners are asked to complete specific language tasks. These tasks foster communication and determine the roles that both the teacher and the learner have to play in the language classroom. The language teacher plays two new main roles: the support person and the planner. Similarly, the roles of the language learner are one of the information finder and the co-worker. Language learners are no longer only receptive individuals, as with these new roles, they become more actively responsible for their learning.

In the example (Figure 5.2) the language teacher has the necessary information to complete the task as he/she plays the role of the support person. The teacher is willing to supply the information but only when the language learner takes the responsibility for gathering the information needed to complete the task. The role of the learner is not simply the one of the listener anymore.

Communication is the interpretation, expression and negotiation of meaning (see Chapter 7 for a more detailed discussion about the role and nature of communication) in a given context for a specific purpose. In a non-classroom setting, conversations are not directed by an individual. Communication is a give-and-take exercise and contributors come from all sides.

> **In a Nutshell ...**
>
> Communication can be defined as the interpretation, expression and negotiation of meaning in each context and for a specific purpose.

**Figure 5.2** Support person and information finder.

**What house is it?** Look over the brochure with a list of houses, getting a view of the different places available to buy in terms of size, price and location. Your teacher will read a description of one of the houses on the list. Listen carefully and try to identify the right one.

Model: (You hear) This house has four rooms.

If you cannot identify the house, then you should ask any or all of the following questions, depending on what you did not understand.

What size did you say?

How many rooms, please?

Can you tell me the price?

Can you specify the location?

**Figure 5.3** Planner and co-worker.

**Phase 1. Assumptions**

**Step 1.** In a small group, prepare a list of what you assume gaining knowledge from books and gaining knowledge from experience consists of. (Fill in the table.)

|   | Knowledge from books | Knowledge from experience |
|---|---|---|
| 1 |   |   |
| 2 |   |   |
| 3 |   |   |
| 4 |   |   |
| 5 |   |   |

**Phase 2. Perspectives**

**Step 2.** As a group, what do you believe is more effective? Tick your choice:

____ Gaining knowledge from books.

____ Gaining knowledge from experience.

**Step 3.** In your group, state several reasons why you think gaining knowledge from *books* is an advantage or disadvantage.

1.

2.

3.

4.

**Step 4.** In your group, state several reasons why you think gaining knowledge from *experience* is an advantage or disadvantage.

1.

2.

3.

4.

**Phase 3. Conclusions**

**Step 5.** What do you think?

Do you think you gain knowledge from books and experience in the same way? Do you think they are two different processes?

Do you think gaining knowledge from reading books is more effective?

Do you think gaining knowledge from experience is more effective?

In the example below (Figure 5.3) the language teacher plays the part of the planner as he/she sets up the different steps of a language task and the language learner becomes the co-worker in the task by interacting, negotiating and expressing meaning to complete the language task.

**Figure 5.4** Open-ended discussion.

**Phase 1. Association**

What do you associate with the phrase 'gaining knowledge from books'?

What do you associate with the phrase 'gaining knowledge from experience'?

**Phase 2. Gaining knowledge**

How can you gain knowledge from books?

How can you gain knowledge from experience?

**Phase 3. Conclusions**

Do you think you gain knowledge from books and experience in the same way? Do you think they are two different processes?

Do you think gaining knowledge from reading books is more effective?

Do you think gaining knowledge from experience is more effective?

---

A more traditional and non-communicative version of the same activity is presented in Figure 5.4 below.

An open-ended discussion is not designed for language learners to learn about the topic or from each other. It is simply a speaking exercise, and speaking cannot be equated to communication. In Figure 5.3, the language task is literally divided into five steps to bring out the layers of communication and assist language learners in tackling the topic. The teacher, whose role is that of the planner, is responsible for designing and planning the task. However, the teacher is not responsible for the final product, as language learners are the co-workers in this task and they are ultimately responsible for its completion.

> **Transcripts and task:** Create two activities for your classroom teaching. In one activity the teacher is the support person and language learners play the role of information finders.
>
> In the other activity, the teacher plays the role of the planner and language learners of the co-workers.

> **Transcripts and task** In this task you should look at the two transcripts from two classrooms, one using a traditional approach to teaching and

the other a communicative one. You have to use the grid to check off whether certain things are happening in the interaction from both the point of view of the teacher and the students. Before you start reading the transcripts study the definitions of the categories provided below.

ERROR CORRECTION (correcting grammatical errors)

GENUINE QUESTIONS (ask questions to which students do not know the answer in advance)

DISPLAY QUESTIONS (type of questions asked to make students display knowledge)

NEGOTIATION OF MEANING (efforts made by both teachers and students to understand the interaction)

(Transcripts from Spada, N., & Lightbown, P. (1993). *How languages are learned.* CUP (pp. 74–7)).

T = teacher

S = student

## Classroom A

T: OK, we finished the book – we finished in the book Chapters 1, 2, 3. Finished Workbooks 1, 2, 3. So today we're going to start with Chapter 4. Don't take your books yet, don't take your books. In 1, 2, 3 we worked in what tense? What tense did we work on? OK?

S: Past

T: In the past – What auxiliary in the past?

S: Did

T: Did (writes on board '1–2-3 Past'). Chapter 4, Chapter 4, we're going to work in the present, present progressive, present continuous – OK? You don't know what it is?

S: Yes

T: Yes? What is it?

S: Little bit

T: A little bit

S: …

T: Eh?

S: Uh, present continuous

T: Present continuous? What's that?

S: e-n-g

T: i-n-g

S: Yes

T: What does that mean, present continuous? You don't know? OK, fine. What are you doing, Paul?

S: Rien

T: Nothing?

S: Rien – nothing

T: You're not doing anything? You're doing something!

S: Not doing anything.

T: You're doing something!

S: Not doing anything.

T: You're doing something – Are, are you listening to me? Are you talking with Marc? What are you doing?

S: No, no—uh—listen—uh—

T: Eh?

S: To you

T: You're you're listening to me.

S: Yes

T: Oh – (writes 'What are you doing? I'm listening to you' on the board).

S: Je—

T: What are you—? You're excited.

S: Yes

T: You're playing with your eraser – (writes 'I'm playing with my eraser' on the board). Would you close the door please, Bernard? Claude, what is he doing?

S: Close the door

T: He is closing the door – (writes 'He's closing the door' on the board) What are you doing, Mario?

S: Moi, I listen to you.

T: You're listening to me.

S: Yes

T: OK. Are you sleeping or are you listening to me?

S: I don't – moitié-moitié, half and half.

T: Half and half, half sleeping, half listening.

## Classroom B

S: It bugs me when a bee sting me.

T: Oh, when a bee stings me.

S: Stings me.

T: Do you get stung often? Does that happen often? The bee stinging many times?

S: Yeah?

T: Often? (Teacher turns to students who aren't paying attention). OK. Sandra and Benoît, you may begin working on a research project, hey? (Teacher turns her attention back to 'What bugs me').

S: It bugs me (inaudible) and my sister put on my clothes.

T: Ah! She – borrows your clothes? When you're older, you may appreciate it because you can switch clothes, maybe. (Teacher turns to check another student's written work) Mélanie, this is yours, I will check. – OK. It's good.

S: It bugs me when I'm sick and my brother doesn't help me – my – my brother, 'cause he – me –

T: OK. You know – when (inaudible) sick, you're sick at home in bed and you say, oh, to your brother or your sister: 'Would you please get me a drink of water?' – 'Ah! Drop dead!' you know, 'Go play in the traffic!' You know, it's not very nice. Martin!

S: It bugs me to have –

T: It bugs me. It bugzz me.

S: It bugs me when my brother takes my bicycle. Every day.

T: Every day? Ah! Doesn't your bro – (inaudible) his bicycle? Could his brother lend his bicycle? Uh, your brother doesn't have a bicycle?

S: Yeah! A new bicycle (inaudible) bicycle.

T: Ah, well. Talk to your mom and dad about it. Maybe negotiate a new bicycle for your brother.

S: (inaudible)

T: He has a new bicycle. But his brother needs a new one too.

S: Yes!

T: Hey, whoa, just a minute! Jean?

S: Martin's brother has –

T: Martin, who has a new bicycle? You or your brother?

S: My brother.

T: And you have an old one.

S: (inaudible)

T: And your brother takes your old one?

S: – clutch – (inaudible) bicycle

T: His bicycle! Ah! How old is your brother?

S: March 23.

T: His birthday?

S: Yeah!

T: And how old was he?

S: Fourteen.

T: Fourteen. Well, why don't you tell your brother that when he takes your bike you will take his bike. And he may have more scratches than he figures for. OK?

| Categories | Teacher | Student |
| --- | --- | --- |
| Errors | | |
| Feedback On Error | | |
| Genuine Question | | |
| Display Questions | | |
| Negotiation of Meaning | | |

# How Do We Learn and Teach Vocabulary?

When language teachers introduce vocabulary to learners, it is not common for them to be asked to repeat words and phrases out loud immediately after they hear them. There is a belief that choral repetition is a successful technique for vocabulary learning (remember the view of Behaviourism!). However, research evidence is showing that choral repletion does not work.

> **Task:** Please read: Wong, W., & Barcroft, J. (2020). Repeat after me or not? Repetition and L2 vocabulary learning. *Foreign Language* Annals, *53*, 64–73. Read both study 1 and study 2 and write about the following:
> - The main purpose of the studies
> - The design of the studies
> - The materials and procedures used to collect and analyse data
> - The results and significance of the two studies

In traditional grammar teaching, the teaching of vocabulary is separated from the teaching of grammar. The assumption is that L2 learners should know the words of a language and its rules. However, rules are not the starting point for language learning. Let's examine what a word is. A word like 'car' has some phonological properties (/kɑː/), syntactical properties (it is a noun and is not more than one) and semantic properties (it is a vehicle with four wheels). Processing words involves making single-form-meaning connections after multiple exposures to input. Language learning is not about learning rules but words!!

> ### Reflect on This ...
> 
> Morphemes such as *-ed-* or third-person singular *-s-* are acquired as part of words and phrases and not in isolation. What needs to be learned are many different words and the ability to make words. Language learning is not about learning morphemes but the words which they are part of.
> 
> What are the pedagogical implications of these statements?

The past two decades of empirical research in L2 learning have been marked by increased interest in vocabulary learning and greater acknowledgement of the importance of vocabulary learning as a central component in the overall learning of a second language. Research on vocabulary learning has addressed a wide variety of issues, ranging from incidental vocabulary learning to the nature of the lexicon system, and how words are processed in the input.

> ## What the Research Is Telling Us …
>
> Fact 1: Research indicates that much of what we refer to as 'grammar knowledge' actually resides in connections between words and their meaning/s. These connections are developed over time based on the exposure to input.
>
> Fact 2: The ability to use language depends on processing individual words and combinations of words over a period of time.

Incidental vocabulary learning refers to learners acquiring new words from context without intending to do so, such as picking up new words during free reading. Language learners do pick up new words while reading texts without any instruction. At the same time, enhancing vocabulary in the input facilitates language learning. Word enhancement (e.g. underlining, bolding or increasing the font size of individual words in the input) is a successful pedagogical intervention that causes certain words to stand out so that language learners may pay more attention to them.

Lexical input processing refers to how language learners process words to which they are exposed. For a word to be learned incidentally or intentionally, a learner must attain access to the form and meaning. Studies on lexical input processing have focused on how learners allocate limited processing resources to different aspects of the vocabulary learning process, such as word form, word meaning and form-meaning connections. Two main findings in this area have indicated that vocabulary learning can be negatively affected by excessive focus on grammatical forms or by forced output such as requiring learners to write new L2 words in sentences.

Based on existing research on the traditional limited role of vocabulary repetition, the following pedagogical suggestions would be more beneficial in promoting effective vocabulary learning in the language classroom:

1. presenting language learners with input in a way that is conducive to effective lexical input processing;
2. presenting new words frequently in the input (there's a lot of research evidence suggesting that frequency of exposure to individual words in a meaningful context is really useful);
3. promoting incidental vocabulary learning. Incidental vocabulary learning occurs when learners pick up new words by being exposed to the same words repeatedly through input flood (flood the input with the same word and encourage word meaning connection);
4. Introducing new words in the context of comprehensible and meaningful input;
5. presenting new words in an enhanced manner. Most research on input enhancement has – to date at least – has focused on enhancement for the acquisition of grammatical forms in a second language (see Chapter 7), but there is some growing body of research indicating that enhancements can also facilitate vocabulary learning;
6. limiting tasks that require language learners to produce language;
7. increasing from less demanding to more demanding tasks gradually.

Language teachers would need to plan how to foster vocabulary learning in the language classroom in a careful way. In traditional instruction, vocabulary is often learned by heart and there is the time assigned for learning specific words. In a more communicative and input-based approach to language instruction, all words and lexical items would need to be presented in the input in a frequent and repeated manner, and opportunities to make word-meaning connections should be regularly provided to language learners.

## Reflect on This ...

How do you think vocabulary is taught in the language classroom?

Based on what we said about vocabulary learning and teaching what are your practical suggestions to introduce new vocabulary in the language classrooms? Identify three!

1.
2.
3.

To make vocabulary easy to understand and process, language teachers might consider presenting vocabulary using pictures to clarify meaning, providing definitions of words or giving learners a list of words to familiarize themselves before the beginning of a language task. Language teachers should also ensure that vocabulary is used within a meaningful context where the input is simplified and easy to comprehend. Words can be enhanced in the input to facilitate comprehension. In the language activity below, the plan is to ensure that language learners become familiar with certain words and expressions.

Vocabulary activity

**Step 1**. Working in pair, jot a list of a few things that you and your classmate usually do in the summer holidays.

**Step 2**. Write down a few sentences about activities you often do during the week. Leave a blank after each one.

EXAMPLE: I go to the seaside every day _____

Sometimes I go fishing _____
I never build sandcastles _____
I rarely explore rock pools_____

**Step 3**. Ask other classmates to see if they do the same thing or different things. If so, get that person's signature in the blank. If not, move on to someone else but note down what your classmate does instead.

**Step 4**. Using the expressions that you have learned, indicate how often you do the following activities in the summer. The last items indicate that you should come up with two activities, not on the list.

EXAMPLE: I never read.
scuba diving
snorkelling
water surfing
kayaking
swimming
getting tanned
playing football
_____
_____

In each of the steps, the task requires language learners to use language in a specific way. Vocabulary instruction should keep in mind the following guidelines: (1) present new words repeatedly and frequently in the input; (2) use meaning-bearing comprehensible input when processing new words; (3) present words in an enhanced manner. Vocabulary tasks should be input-oriented.

# Three Principles of Effective Vocabulary Teaching

In general terms, the three main principles discussed here emphasize the provision of input and opportunities for input processing as positive driving forces in vocabulary learning. The three principles discussed here highlight how presenting vocabulary in the input and giving learners adequate opportunities to process new words are critical steps in effective vocabulary teaching and learning in the language classroom.

## Language Teachers Should Present New Words Frequently and Repeatedly in the Input

Language teachers need to keep in mind the importance for learners to process (assign meaning) and comprehend new words in the input. Immediately requiring language learners to use new words in a language task before allowing them to process these new words in the input is inconsistent with how vocabulary is acquired. Before learners can use target words, they need to process the new words in the input and make a word-meaning connection. Vocabulary can be introduced using pictures or drawings, by pointing to and discussing real-world items or by providing definitions of target words and expressions. Vocabulary can also be presented in the classroom during discussions or within reading comprehension texts.

## Language Teachers Should Use Comprehensible and Meaningful Input When Presenting New Words

> **In a Nutshell …**
>
> Vocabulary learning takes place when teachers allow learners to process and comprehend new words in the input before they are involved in the production of new words.

Language teachers must introduce language learners to new words through comprehensible and meaningful input. Language learning largely depends on language learners having access to meaningful and comprehensible input. Input needs to convey meaning and be sufficiently comprehensible so that language learners can attach the form to meaning, and in the case of vocabulary learning, to attach new word forms to appropriate word meanings.

Modifying input in ways that render it more comprehensible can help to promote vocabulary learning. Some techniques that can be used to make input more comprehensible are speaking at a slower pace, using visuals to help convey meaning, using short sentences, repeating sentences and individual words, paraphrasing, using gestures and providing multiple examples. Comprehension checks in the form of 'yes' or 'no' questions may also be useful to confirm whether learners are comprehending new words in the language classroom.

## Language Teachers Should Limit Forced Output at the Initial Stages of Learning New Words

Language teachers must limit vocabulary production (oral and written) by learners at the initial stages of learning new words in the target language. To learn new words, learners need to allocate processing resources towards (1) encoding new words and (2) making word-meaning connections. Requiring learners to exhaust processing resources for output tasks may inhibit their ability to process and assign meaning to new words. When presented with the target words, learners must make use of limited mental resources to begin to encode the target word forms, activate word meanings, and make appropriate connections between word and meaning. Tasks that involve forced output may inhibit this ability. At later stages, activities that involve more elaboration on the meaning and production of the new words can be gradually developed.

**Quiz:** Take the following short quiz to see what you have learned since the last quiz. You can circle more than one option.

1. The role of the language teacher in the classroom is of the…

    a) Leader
    b) Facilitator
    c) Architect

2. The role of the language learner in the classroom is of the…

    a) Parrot
    b) Negotiator
    c) Co-builder

3. You learn vocabulary through…

   a. Repetition
   b. Learning words by heart
   c. Use of vocabulary in a meaningful context

4. You teach vocabulary by…

   a. Providing new words and meaning
   b. Translating new words
   c. Providing new words in the context of a task

## Task: Enact the Role of the Planner as a Language Teacher in the Classroom

Part 1: Working in small groups, select one of the following sets of discussion questions and create an activity consisting of a series of steps (3–4).

- What do you think about 'smoking'? Is it harmful? Is it difficult to overcome? What measures would you introduce to completely ban it?
- What do you think about the role of social media in society? Too intrusive? What measures would you introduce to regulate this?

Part 2: Write your planned activity and share it with the other groups.

Part 3: Evaluate your activity with the other groups on the following:

- What role do the teacher and learners play?
- Do all learners participate and contribute to complete the activity?

## Takeaways from This Chapter

- Repetition does not increase vocabulary acquisition.
- Repetition is not an effective method in vocabulary instruction.

- The presentation of new vocabulary without access to meaning does not facilitate the acquisition.
- The presentation of vocabulary in a comprehensible and meaningful way might facilitate the acquisition.
- Vocabulary must be easy to understand and process.
- Language instructors might consider presenting vocabulary using pictures to clarify meaning.
- Language teachers should ensure that vocabulary is used in a meaningful context where the input is simplified and easy to comprehend.
- Words can be enhanced in the input to facilitate comprehension and processing.

In designing a vocabulary task, language instructors should follow this general guideline:

- Carefully design a task considering the vocabulary needed to complete the task.
- Design meaningful and interactive tasks.
- Present target vocabulary frequently in the input.
- Increase the difficulty of tasks involving target vocabulary over time.
- Focus on interpretation and comprehension activities first before moving to output practice.

## Task: Presenting Vocabulary through Input

Introducing vocabulary through input is like introducing vocabulary in context. What type of strategies would you suggest using in the language classroom to allow learners to learn words in context?

_____
_____
_____
_____

## Knowing More about the Subject

Barcroft, J. (2012). *Input-based incremental vocabulary instruction*. TESOL International Association.

Barcroft, J. (2018). *Vocabulary in language teaching*. Routledge.

Benati, A. (2020). *Key questions in language teaching*. Cambridge University Press.

Bybee, J. L. (1991). Natural morphology: The organization of paradigms and language acquisition. In C. Ferguson & T. Huebner (eds), *Second language acquisition and linguistic theory* (pp. 67–91). John Benjamins.

Coady, J., & Huckin, T. (2012). *Second language vocabulary acquisition*. Cambridge University Press.

Fitchtner, F., & Barcroft, J. (2021). Effective treatment of vocabulary when teaching L2 reading: The example of Yoko Tawada's *Wo Europa anfängt*. *Reading in Foreign Language, 33*, 263–77.

Jackendoff, R., & Audring, J. (2020). *The texture of the lexicon: Relational morphology and the parallel architecture* (pp. 132–67). Oxford University Press.

Jordan, G., & Long, M. (2022). *English language teaching now and how it could be*. Cambridge Scholars Publishing.

Lee, J., & VanPatten, B. (2003). *Making communicative language teaching happen*. McGraw-Hill.

Meara, P. (2009). *Words associations and second language vocabulary acquisition*. John Benjamins.

Nation, I. S. P. (2022). *Learning vocabulary in another language*. Cambridge University Press.

Wong, W., & Barcroft, J. (2020). Repeat after me or not? Repetition and L2 vocabulary learning. *Foreign Language Annals, 53*, 64–73.

## Further Clarifications

In this section, we aim to further clarify some of the terms or concepts presented in the chapter.

**Behaviourism** was a theory in strong opposition to Chomsky's view of language and language acquisition that argued that humans have an innate language knowledge and that they are genetically programmed to develop their linguistic system in certain specific ways. Behaviourism maintained that it is the learners' experience which is largely responsible for language learning and this is more important that any innate capacity.

**The Audiolingual Method** emphasized the use of memorization, mechanical and pattern drills practice. The main principles of The Audiolingual Method were that learners are exposed to correct models/patterns of the target L2. Language learners have to repeat, manipulate or transform a particular form or structure.

**The Grammar Translation Method** assumes that language acquisition develops as language learners develop the ability to read a text in another language and to translate that text from one language into another. The ability to communicate using the target language was not the main goal for language teaching.

# 6

# How Do We Make Language Classrooms Input-Rich?

Overview  91

What Is Language Input? And How Do We Provide Effective Input in the Classroom?  92

How Do We Provide Effective Interaction in the Classroom?  101

How Do We Develop Communicative Interactive Speaking Tasks?  103

Knowing More about the Subject  109

## Overview

In this chapter how we can make input comprehensible (easy to process) and meaningful in the language classroom will be discussed, providing specific examples. Input is a basic ingredient for language learning. So, what does input mean in the context of learning a language? Input is the language that learners hear or see in a communicative context. Language teachers should provide learners with level-appropriate input and interaction. The role of input often gets lip service in language teaching. The main aim of this chapter is to explore three questions (Figure 6.1).

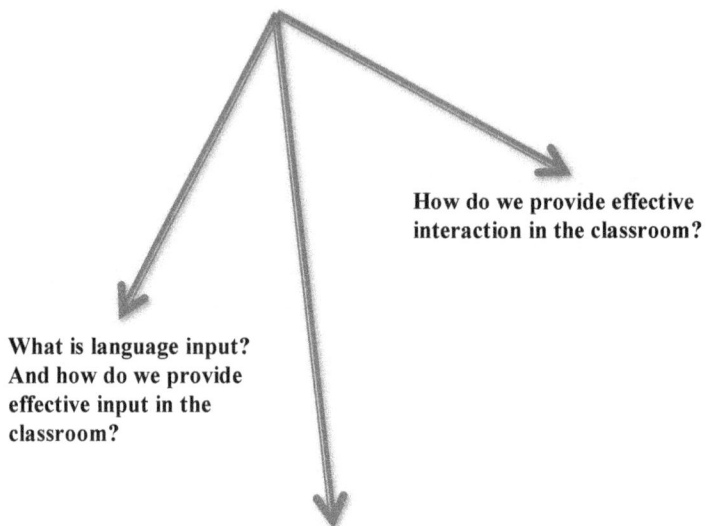

**Figure 6.1** Key questions of Chapter 6.

# What Is Language Input? And How Do We Provide Effective Input in the Classroom?

> **Task:** What is input? Please provide your definition

What is input in the context of acquiring a language? Input is the language that learners hear or read and carries a specific meaning that we need to understand. Language learners must comprehend the meaning of the language input they are exposed to. Learners have to use the information they have comprehended for practical and meaningful use. For example, when we are looking for a place to eat and we need to stop someone to ask for help, we would say something like *excuse me, do you know where I can find a good restaurant nearby?* The passerby would hopefully provide us with the necessary information to find a good restaurant. We would then use this information to go from where we are to the restaurant.

> **In a Nutshell ...**
>
> Input for the purpose of learning must be comprehensible and meaningful.

In contrast to the above meaningful exchange of information, in the language classroom, we often hear language teachers asking learners to repeat a word, providing explicit information about grammatical rules or explaining something which language learners might need to memorize. Language learners are very often engaged in activities where they need to repeat the language without knowing what they are saying. They perform some kind of language exercise mechanically without understanding the real meaning of the language used. In the example below the language teacher provides a language model for repetition. The learner produces the language mechanically without necessarily comprehending the meaning. This kind of practice does not lead to language learning.

1. Instructor: *I love Italian food*
2. Learner: *I love* Italian food (repetition)

Input for acquisition is the language that is embedded in a communicative context that language learners must attend to for its meaning. Learners acquire a second language mainly through exposure to comprehensible, meaningful input, in a similar manner as they acquire their first language.

> **What the Research Is Telling Us about First and Second Language Learning ...**
>
> Fact 1: Language learners follow natural orders in acquiring morphemes.
> Fact 2: Input plays a primary role.

> Fact 3: The processes and mechanisms responsible for language learning are similar.
>
> Fact 4: The potential differences between learning a first language and learning a second language can only be attributed to external factors such as the quantity and quality of input learners received.
>
> Fact 5: In acquiring their first language, children have full access to innate mechanisms. Adults, however, may not have access to the same mechanisms when learning a second language.
>
> Fact 6: In acquiring a second language, adults are not exposed to the same quantity and quality of input.

The input that language learners receive should be simplified with the use of contextual and extra-linguistic clues to make it easier to comprehend and process it. Comprehending language means understanding the meaning of the input we are exposed to. Processing language means being able to connect a word or form with its meaning. For example, the word 'house' is connected to 'a space where someone lives and has four walls and a ceiling'. The verb 'play' is connected to the meaning 'engage in sport and recreation activities'.

Language learners should be exposed to comprehensible input, and they should be provided with opportunities to focus on meaning rather than only practising specific grammatical forms, such as textbook grammar rules.

> ## Reflect on This ... Which of the Following Examples Is Input for Acquisition?
>
> A) My wife loves pets. She has four dogs and two cats ... next weekend she wants to buy a few extra puppies ... we have now many pets and we would need to buy a bigger house to fit them all...
>
> B) In English, the simple past tense (regular verbs) is formed by adding the suffix -ed to the stem of the verb.

> **Task:** What is good input? How do you describe how input works in language learning?
>
> Can you think about your language experiences and provide examples of input you found …
>
> Comprehensible:
>
> Incomprehensible:

Simplified input is language input that is easier to process. Language teachers should use high-frequency vocabulary which is easier to comprehend by learners (see Chapter 2 to see how vocabulary learning can be facilitated in the language classroom). They can also make use of gestures, pictures or drawings to make input simpler and easy to comprehend and process The use of short sentences can reduce the burden of processing (making form/word-meaning connections) and increases comprehension.

> **In a Nutshell …**
>
> Input for learning is the language which we read or hear and conveyed a message we need to attend.

Good input language for learning is not the explanation about grammar, memorization of vocabulary and mechanical practice. Effective input language is about creating opportunities for language learners to hear or read the language in a communicative context that they need to process for meaning. Engaging language learners in communication means creating opportunities for them to interpret, negotiate and express meaning for a purpose in a specific context. Language teaching should focus on providing learners with a rich variety of comprehensible input and opportunities to use language spontaneously and meaningfully. Interaction offers opportunities for the negotiation of meaning and language learning.

Quality input has two characteristics:

1. Needs to be at an appropriate level;
2. Learners are engaged with the input, which means they interact with it.

> **In a Nutshell ...**
>
> Good quality input needs to be at the appropriate level of the L2 learners and they need to be given the opportunity for interaction.

Language learners do not comprehend everything they hear or read as they can't attach meaning to all the language they are exposed to. Language learning consists of the unconscious mapping of meaning and corresponding form during comprehension.

Language learners acquire language through comprehension, but they don't simply absorb everything they hear or read. Their language systems process, organize and store language data continuously interacting with input and internal mechanisms (e.g. input-processing strategies) responsible for how language is processed. We refer to input-processing strategies as mechanisms in our mind responsible for processing information during exposure to input (more later in this chapter). To make its way through the system, the input must be simplified and made easy to comprehend. Input must be anchored in something concrete, and its content makes it comprehensible with the use of linguistic and non-linguistic means (e.g. pictures, cartoons, gestures). Language learners should be constantly involved in interaction with each other.

> **Reflect on This ...**
>
> How would you use the target language with L2 learners who do not have any knowledge about the new language?
>
> Can you provide a few practical examples?
>
> What other means would you consider?

TEACHER: My name is John, What is your name?
STUDENT: [pause]
TEACHER: What is your name? Are you Mike? Paul? What is your name?
STUDENT: Oh, uh, Nick.
TEACHER: Thanks. (say hello to somebody else) Hello. My name is John. What is your name?
STUDENT: Uh, Frank.
TEACHER: Right. (to all classrooms). We have two students. He is Frank and he is Nick.

There are four features in the above exchanges that should consider making input language easy to understand and process.

- Short sentences (e.g. the simpler syntax is easy to process)
- Slower rate (e.g. extra stress in nouns makes input easy to process)
- Rephrasing (e.g. interactions offer opportunities for negotiation)
- Content is clear (e.g. easy language input is more processable)

## Consider This ...

Do language learners understand every word they hear or read? Is this crucial?

**Task:** In groups examine the characteristic of simplified input. Is there one of particular importance? Use of simple sentences? Frequent and simpler vocabulary?

1.

2.

3.

One of the questions raised by language teachers is: How can we use the target language with beginners? After all, beginners can't understand! Language teachers must simplify their language as a natural part of making themselves understood. They can make use of non-linguistic means: such as drawings, photos, diagrams, objects gestures and visual aids to accompany speech. They can make language modifications to ensure that the features of the target language are more salient. They can use familiar topics for the learners so that they have some background knowledge and it is easier for them to comprehend the language.

> **Task:** Provide a specific example of how we make input comprehensible and message-oriented ...
>
> Comprehensible:
>
> Message-oriented:

> **Quiz**
>
> Take the following short quiz to see what you have learned so far in this module. Answers are provided at the end.
>
> 1. Input can be modified ...
>
>     a. By simplifying syntax
>     b. By reading aloud
>     c. By explaining rules
>
> 2. What is the best example of effective input for language learning?
>
>     a. Providing explicit information
>     b. Engaging learners with message-oriented input
>     c. Read and repeat
>
> 3. How do you make input comprehensible?
>
>     a. Use gestures and pictures
>     b. Explain meaning
>     c. Provide translation of words

## What the Research Is Telling Us ...

- Fact 1: Input is central to language classroom learning.
- Fact 2: Input must be simplified, comprehensible and processable to be learned.
- Fact 3: Input must be message-oriented to affect learning.
- Fact 4: Only a small portion of the input becomes intake.
- Fact 5: Interaction facilitates the learning of lexical words and their meanings.
- Fact 6: Interaction has a facilitative role in terms of language learning.

The role of input in L2 learning has been investigated from three main perspectives: (1) input processing, (2) connectionism, (3) interaction. All these perspectives have the following elements in common: Input is a key and basic ingredient in the acquisition of a language.

### In a Nutshell ...

Intake is the data which is processed by learners when exposed to language input.

An input-processing perspective argues that only a small proportion of the language input learners are exposed to is being processed and internalized into our language system. As we said in Chapter 1 that proportion of the input is called intake. When learners process language input and seek to comprehend the meaning, a form-meaning connection is made (one form connects to one meaning at a time). For example, the *-ed* at the end of the verb stem in English means that an action refers to the past.

Developing language learners' competence to map one form to one meaning is essential for language learning. However, this processing is somewhat constrained as learners filter the information they process, using internal processing strategies

### In a Nutshell ...

The use of processing strategies by L2 learners is a constraint in language acquisition.

to help them cope with the amount of information they receive. Language learners use unconsciously two main strategies to cope with the input they are exposed to and select what to process and what not to process: (1) they process input for meaning before they process it for form, (2) they process the first noun they encounter in a sentence as the subject of that sentence.

The first processing strategy helps learners to direct their attention towards content words to understand the main meaning of a sentence. In the sentence 'Yesterday I watched football on TV', learners would process the word *Yesterday* first before the verb ending *-ed* as in *watched*. Language learners would in this case fail to make a connection between the form (past tense ending) and its meaning (the action has taken place in the past). This misprocessing would inevitably cause a delay in language learning as this connection is not made.

The second processing strategy helps learners assign the role of the subject to the first element they encounter in a sentence leading in some cases to the misinterpretation of the meaning of a sentence. Once again this misprocessing would cause a delay in acquisition. An example is a sentence such as 'Jane was kissed by Carl', where L2 learners would interpret the sentence as if it were Jane who kissed Carl.

> **In a Nutshell ...**
>
> The three main perspectives on the role of input in L2 learning are:
>
> - input processing,
> - connectionism,
> - interaction.

The so-called connectionist perspective argues that input plays a key role in language learning in terms of providing multiple cues for learners. Learning of appropriate form-meaning connections is driven by several factors, most of which are related to the reliability of a particular cue. The following factors are two of the key elements: (1) frequency, (2) reliability.

Frequency relates to how often a form-meaning connection occurs in the input. If it is frequent, then the cue is strengthened, and learners can rely on it. In terms of reliability, some cues are more reliable than others in helping learners to make a correct interpretation. Language learning takes place as learners make associations and these associations gradually grow to form a kind of language network (e.g. play is connected to played and both are associated with the word player).

From an interaction perspective, the input can be distinguished as either interactional or non-interactional. Interactional input refers to input received during interaction where there is some kind of communicative exchange involving the learner and at least another person (e.g. a conversation or a classroom discussion). Language learners can negotiate meaning and make some conversational adjustments. This means that conversation and interaction make linguistics features salient to the learner, and negotiation of meaning can facilitate language acquisition. Non-interactional input refers to the kind of input that occurs in the context of non-reciprocal discourse and learners are not part of an interaction (e.g. an announcement at a train station). Conversational interaction and negotiation of meaning can facilitate language learning. In an attempt to facilitate comprehension, one person can ask the other to modify and simplify the language used.

> **Reflect on this:** Please provide a full answer to these three questions: If input must be comprehensible and meaningful, what would 'good input' look like?
>
> Think about some common activities in language classrooms, such as memorizing vocabulary lists of grammar to learn by heart. Does it constitute good input for learners? Why or why not?
>
> In your experience, is rich input usually available in language classrooms?

The lack of knowledge about what good language input leads to misleading claims and misunderstanding among language teachers:

- The claim is that all the input we are exposed to can be comprehended and processed.
- The claim is that exposure to mechanical practice works.
- The claim is that knowing grammar rules facilitates language learning.

In Chapter 8 we will be discussing these issues in more detail.

# How Do We Provide Effective Interaction in the Classroom?

> **Task:** What is interaction? Please provide a brief definition of the term.

Interaction can be defined as situations where there is some kind of communicative exchange involving the learner and at least another person. Through these exchanges, learners have the advantage of being able to negotiate meaning and make some conversational adjustments to comprehend the language. For example, learners sometimes request clarifications if they do not understand the meaning.

Input modifications happen when the other speaker adjusts his or her speech due to perceived difficulties in learner comprehension. The other speaker can also indicate in some way that the learner has produced something non-native-like (the role and nature of corrective feedback will be discussed in Chapter 8).

In terms of negotiation of meaning tools available to learners, the most commonly used are the following:

- Clarification requests can be defined as an expression used to clarify learners' speech (e.g. what did you say?);
- Confirmation checks are used by learners and teachers when it is not clear what has been said (e.g. did I understand correctly …?);
- Comprehension checks are used when one speaker is not convinced that the other speaker has understood what has been said (e.g. did you get it?).

These types of interactional modifications might have positive effects on language learning.

---

**Task:** Can you provide a further example of each of those interaction modifications in English or in another language?

1.

2.

3.

Language teachers should expose learners to comprehensible input and give them the opportunities to communicate, negotiate meaning and interact with each other at all times in the language classroom.

> **In a Nutshell ...**
>
> The three main types of interactional modifications are:
>
> - clarification requests,
> - confirmation checks,
> - comprehension checks.

> **Task:** The centrality of input in the classroom along with research on L2 learning suggests a move away from the traditional syllabus/curriculum with a focus on memorizing vocabulary and grammar chapters. The question is: What would you put in place of these chapters? How would you organize the teaching?
> Can you come up with ten activities you would include?
>
> To get you started, here are three:
>
> - What clothes we wear and why we wear them
> - What food do we eat and whether we have healthy diets
> - Who we tell our problems/secrets to and what we keep to ourselves
>
> Imagine it is the first day of your class. Students come in and are surprised to see you using the target language.
>
> 'Where are the worksheets?', they ask. 'Why aren't we learning tenses?' What would you say to them? How would you explain to students why it is your job to use the second language as much as possible?
>
> Read the next section before you complete this task.

# How Do We Develop Communicative Interactive Speaking Tasks?

Communication involves our competence in interpreting, negotiating and expressing meaning for a specific purpose (more on this in Chapter 7). Interactive tasks provide language learners with opportunities to communicate and exchange information. Expressing meaning is an interactive process involving producing, receiving and processing information. Communicating in another language is not just developing the competence to use grammar correctly, have access to vocabulary and pronounce words correctly (what we call linguistic competence), but also being able to understand when, why and in what ways to produce language (what we call communicative competence).

Language learners must engage in the language classroom with communicative interactive tasks where they use language that is meaningful for a specific purpose. All communicative tasks must ensure learners develop their ability to share information, negotiate meaning and interact with others. Speaking interactive tasks must only be developed to promote communication and communicative language use.

> **In a Nutshell ...**
>
> A language task requires L2 learners:
>
> - to interpret language input and
> - to use language for spontaneous communication and interaction.

In Chapter 7 a more in-depth discussion on the role and nature of communicative tasks will be provided. A task is a classroom interactive activity that has (1) an objective attainable only by interaction among participants, (2) a mechanism for structuring and sequencing interaction and (3) a focus on meaning exchange.

A language task is a learning activity that requires learners to comprehend, negotiate, manipulate and produce the target language as they need to complete a set of communicative steps. Negotiation of meaning refers to the ability to clarify meaning when there is a breakdown of communication between two or more speakers.

In the traditional speaking language classroom, teachers and learners engage using very little language. Language teachers normally ask the so-called display questions (e.g. teachers ask learners, 'Where is my pen?', showing them that the pen is on the table). These types of questions have no communicative purpose apart from displaying already existing knowledge.

Developing effective speaking interactive tasks where learners are guided, supported and, have clear objectives to achieve would reduce their anxieties and increase their motivation. They need to have the opportunity to exchange previously unknown information. Language teachers must develop speaking interactive tasks that stimulate communication in the language classroom. Four key principles need to be kept in mind in developing interactive tasks.

- The first principle relates to the fact that learners are co-workers and they need to engage in exchanging information with other speakers. The teacher is the planner and needs to ensure that plenty of opportunities for interaction, interpretation and expression of meaning are given to language learners during a task.
- The second principle relates to the fact that all learners and not the teacher should dictate these communication exchanges.
- The third principle refers to the fact that learners need to be exposed to comprehensible and meaningful input and that they need to have opportunities for meaningful interactions (pair and group interaction) and language production in the language classroom.

The fourth principle refers to the fact that learners need to engage in interactive meaningful speaking tasks with clear purposes. Learners must be exposed to authentic language to communicate.

> **In a Nutshell ...**
>
> Speaking is an interactive process of constructing meaning that involves producing, receiving, interpreting and processing information.

Five components can be considered as the main guidelines for the development of effective speaking interactive communicative tasks:

1. The importance of establishing the general purpose of the interactive task.
2. The importance of providing input meaningfully (using linguistics and non-linguistic means) and comprehensibly.
3. The importance of establishing how the information is presented and how it is used by language learners.
4. The importance of establishing the procedures for performing the task (e.g. group vs. pair work).
5. The importance of establishing the main outcome/s of the task.

In structuring interactive communicative tasks, language teachers should adopt the following criteria:

- Teachers must determine the main outcome/s of the language task.
- Teachers must determine the sources from which learners assess the information.
- Teachers should break down the topic into subtopics.

- Teachers should create and sequence concrete tasks for learners to complete.
- Teachers should build into the task some linguistic support.

Interactive speaking tasks (see Figure 6.2) should substitute traditional speaking practice in the language classroom where learners would be asked to talk about a specific topic such as 'What did you do at the weekend?' or 'Can you talk about your family?' In this kind of open-ended question activity type, language learners will have very little to talk about and few opportunities to interact with or exchange information. A four-stage approach needs to be considered to avoid using traditional and ineffective open-ended questions.

## Determine the main outcome/s of the task

This is the first criterion to consider in developing an effective interactive communicative speaking task. The main informational goal of the task needs to be determined. In other words, language teachers need to establish what specific questions/activities L2 learners will be able to answer/engage with at the end of the task. What is the desired outcome of the task? What can learners achieve at the end of the task? How would they be able to use the information exchanged with others during the task? These are the questions to keep in mind as you plan the language task.

## Determine the main sources

The information that language learners would need to exchange during the task should generate from several sources: internal (personal views and opinions) and external (e.g. existing texts). In developing and planning an interactive speaking task we need to determine the sources needed by learners to complete the task.

## Break down the topic into subtopics and develop a step-by-step approach

A task is not an open-ended question. In this sense, a task must be developed thinking of the different layers involved in interpreting, negotiating and expressing meaning. Each step would be connected and would contribute to the completion of the language task.

During these steps language learners can use language for meaningful goals.

## Build into the task some language support

Language learners should be provided by the teacher with some language support. What does it mean? It means that learners would need to have language knowledge (words and forms) to complete the task and teachers can provide this support throughout the task.

> **In a Nutshell ...**
>
> Interactive speaking tasks consist of four criteria:
>
> - determine the main outcome/s of the task
> - determine the main sources
> - break down the topic into subtopics and develop a step-by-step approach
> - build into the task some language support

In the interactive task above, language learners can interpret, negotiate and express meaning for a specific purpose. Interactive tasks can be described as one-way or two-way tasks.

**Figure 6.2** Interactive speaking task.

**Step 1.** Using the chart below, fill it in with at least three things that you and your classmate do for Christmas and New Year's Eve.

|  | Me | Classmate |
|---|---|---|
| Christmas |  |  |
| New Year's Eve |  |  |

**Step 2.** Now speak to five or six other classmates and ask similar questions about the two events. The idea is to gather information so that you can write contrasting and comparative statements.

**Step 3.** Using the information obtained in steps 1 and 2 prepare a chart with the different 'habits' of you and your classmates during these two festivities. Establish commonalities and differences in how people celebrate Christmas and New Year's Eve.

**Step 4.** Submit your chart to your language teacher and decide who had more fun.

> **Task:** Create one task for your language teaching where you plan step by step and you keep in mind that language learners need to play a proactive role! This time you would like to know about learners' habits during the week and at the weekend. Remember the four criteria!
> 1. Determine the outcome/s
> 2. Determine the main sources needed to complete the task
> 3. Break down the topic into subtopics and construct a step approach
> 4. Build into the task some language support

## Quiz

Take the following short quiz to see what you have learned so far in this module. You can circle more than one option.

1. An interactive communicative speaking task …
   a. Prepares students to interact
   b. Involves reviewing a grammar point
   c. Practises language

2. A task…
   a. Has always had a communicative purpose
   b. Has a focus on language practice
   c. Both a and b

3. Interaction…
   a. Facilitates acquisition of words
   b. Facilitating the acquisition of formal properties
   c. Both a and b

4. Language learning is…
   a. Intake dependent
   b. Output dependent
   c. Both a and b

5. Input is…
   a. Necessary
   b. Sufficient
   c. Not a key element in language learning

## Takeaways from This Chapter

- Input (comprehensible and meaning-based) and interaction (negotiation of meaning and corrective feedback) are essential ingredients in language learning.
- Tasks must be communicative and interactive.
- A task is a classroom activity that has an objective which can be achieved by interacting with other participants, structuring and sequencing the interaction, and focusing on meaning.
- Interactive speaking tasks should be used in the language classroom instead of traditional oral practice.

**Task:** Read Farzaneh, T., & Benati, A. (2021). Comparing whole-class discussion and task-based activity: A small-scale study, *Instructed Second Language Acquisition, 5*, 1–36.

- What is the main purpose of the study?
- What are the main questions?
- What is the design of the study?
- What are the materials and procedures used?
- What are the main findings?
- What are the main implications?

# Knowing More about the Subject

Benati, A. (2013). *Key issues in second language teaching*. Equinox.
Benati, A. (2022). *Key terms for teachers*. Equinox.
Benati, A., & Angelovska, T. (2016). *Second language acquisition: A theoretical introduction to real-world application*. Bloomsbury.
Bygate, M. (1987). *Speaking*. Oxford University Press.
Ellis, N. (2009). Optimizing the input: Frequency and sampling in usage-based and form-focused learning. In M. Long & C. Doughty (eds), *Handbook of second language acquisition* (pp. 63–103). Blackwell.
Ellis, R. (2003). *Task-based language learning and teaching*. Oxford University Press.

Farzaneh, T., & Benati, A. (2021). Comparing whole-class discussion and task-based activity: A small-scale study, *Instructed Second Language Acquisition, 5*, 1–36.

Lee, J. (2000). *Tasks and communicating in language classrooms.* McGraw-Hill.

Mackey, A. (2010). *Input, Interaction, and corrective feedback in L2 learning.* Oxford University Press.

Piske, T., & Young-Scholten, N. (2009). *Input matters in SLA.* Multilingual Matters.

VanPatten, B. (2003). *From input to output.* McGraw-Hill.

# Further Clarifications …

In this section, we aim to further clarify some of the terms or concepts presented in the chapter.

**Form-meaning connection** in this chapter refers to the correspondence between the formal properties of language and the meaning they encode. The word 'bike' corresponds to the meaning of a vehicle with two wheels.

**Frequency** in this chapter refers to the relative frequency of formal features in the language that people hear or read. For example, *a* is a highly frequent grammatical form in English whereas the past participle *sought* is much less frequent.

# 7

# How Do We Develop Communication in the Language Classroom?

Overview  111

What Is the Nature and Role of Communication?  113

   Expression and Interpretation of the Meaning  113

   Context  114

   Purpose  114

How to Develop an Effective Writing Task?  116

   An Interactive Approach to Writing  121

   The Pre-Writing Stage  123

   The Writing Stage  124

   Language Focus Stage  124

   Free-Writing Activity  125

Free-Writing Task: The Life of Albert Einstein  126

   Collaborative Writing  126

Knowing More about the Subject  129

## Overview

In traditional teaching, lesson objectives are reduced to the ability for learners to complete a chapter in a language textbook or learn a set of vocabulary or a grammatical feature of the target language. In many cases, a lesson objective is equated with the learning and practising of grammar.

Traditional classroom practice is structured around the learning of a particular form (e.g. complete the story with the right form, write one sentence for each of the drawings in the story and the like). Very often language teachers make use of Q/A to measure whether learners can use the information and knowledge gained during a lesson. Despite the attempt of the teacher to extract information, Q/A practice very often resolves in the following: (1) few learners participate, (2) native speaker speaks a lot, (3) roles for both the teacher and the learner are restricted, (4) learners speak very little, (5) not much interaction and negotiation of meaning takes place in the language classroom.

Communication is not equivalent to questions and answers (Q/A) practice. Communication can be defined as the expression, interpretation and negotiation of meaning. We know that interaction promotes comprehension and comprehension promotes acquisition. Effective language tasks can promote learning (see also Chapter 9) and provide a purpose for language use. A task can be used to achieve a specific lesson objective. Interactive language tasks, and not mechanical exercises, should form the backbone of the curriculum. Lots of classroom teaching is dominated by the PPP approach as discussed in Chapter 3. One reason for this is that teachers don't understand what their options are, what is truly communicative and interactive in terms of activities in class. A definition and understanding of the nature and role of communication is a key principle in developing an understanding of contemporary language teaching.

In this chapter two questions will be addressed (Figure 7.1).

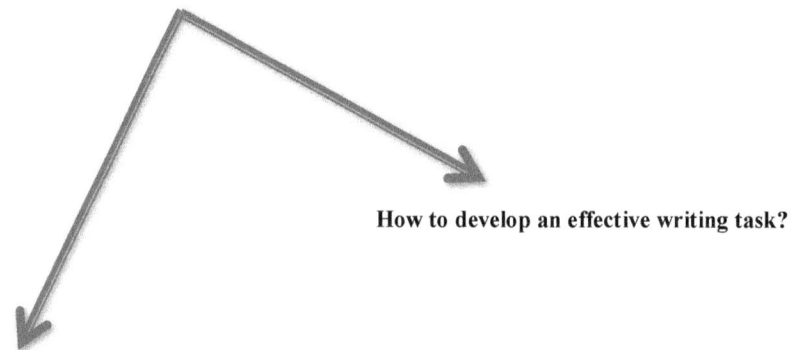

**Figure 7.1** Key questions of Chapter 7.

# What Is the Nature and Role of Communication?

> **Task:** What is communication? Please provide your definition.

Communication is the expression, interpretation and negotiation of meaning in a given context for a specific purpose. Communication has a specific purpose. Let's define each of these components.

## Expression and Interpretation of the Meaning

The expression refers to learners' language production. People can communicate meaning with or without language (e.g. by raising eyebrows, smiling, waving and eyes narrowing). In face-to-

> **In a Nutshell ...**
>
> Communication is the expression, interpretation and negotiation of meaning in a given context.

face interactions, people tend to use both oral and non-oral expressions of meaning. Communication is not one-sided, and there is always someone else expected to understand the message or intent we would like to communicate. There is always at least one person who would need to comprehend and interpret the message intended. In addition, when we fail to communicate something effectively, people seek to negotiate meaning in an attempt to understand the message conveyed. Negotiation of meaning shows up in a variety of ways:

> Statement: 'Sorry, I don't get it' 'Can you please say that again?'
> Comprehension check: 'Did you get it?' 'I am not sure you understood?'
> Confirmation check: 'Let me see if I fully understand. You're saying that…'

All of these reactions (including gestures) and others are ways in which interlocutors initiate meaning checks. They are forms of negotiation of meaning which can lead to a full and better interpretation of meaning.

Meaning refers to the information contained in some kind of message. If someone says, for example, '*I am tired*' the literal message is that the person is tired. But meaning can also refer to a speaker's intent. Maybe the person who says '*I am tired*' is worried that someone else is planning to invite him out.

> **Task:** What do you think is easier: Expression or interpretation of meaning?

## Context

The construct of context refers to two principal aspects of communication: (1) the setting and (2) the participants. When people speak, write, listen or read, they do so with a purpose. Context is a powerful dimension of any communicative event. Context constrains how people communicate. Being in a language classroom with a teacher and a group of other learners, for example, is not the same thing as being at a local restaurant with your friends. Interacting with your lawyer in an office is not the same as interacting with your family at home. As context shifts, the nature of communication inevitably changes.

## Purpose

People communicate for a purpose. We don't use language or gestures or signs or anything else involved in communication without a reason. In everyday life, these two major purposes of communication overlap and we often move back and forth between the two during an interaction. People generally use language for the following purposes:

- The social purpose is to establish and maintain relationships between people. We often interact with other people and friends to ask how

someone is doing, or to plan to go out, and for many other social purposes.
- The informational purpose is to learn something new about other people, and more in general to obtain information.

> **In a Nutshell ...**
>
> What transpires in language practice is not communication.

Communication between two or more entities always has some purpose. When we use language with each other during a communicative event, we don't use language for the sake of using language. We use language to get something done or to let someone know something. In many language classrooms what very often language teachers do is language practice and not communication. In traditional language classrooms, for example, learners engage in a practice that involves repetition, open-ended questions type and the transformation of sentences. Does the following look familiar to you?

Transform the sentence using the past tense.

1. I play football with my friends
2. I _____ football with my friends

How about the following open-ended question?

What do you do in your free time?

All language textbooks are full practice which looks like the ones above. This type of language practice is not communicative at all! If teachers and learners are not engaged in genuine expression and interpretation of meaning in a specific context and for a specific purpose, what they're doing does not equate to communication.

In the first sample of practice above, the learner is mechanically transforming the sentence from present tense to past tense. The practice is so mechanical that even if we had inserted a nonsense word, the learner would have still inserted the correct past tense in the sentence. This practice lacks any communicative purpose. The sole purpose of the practice is to produce a correct form in the past. Learners and teachers are not expressing, negotiating or interpreting any meaning.

In the example of the open-ended question, there are no opportunities for the learner to interpret or negotiate the meaning. When teachers ask these types of questions normally only a few students in the classroom venture an answer. Learners might say 'I go to the gym', and another learner says 'I go to the cinema'. Learners would not say much and would not pay much attention to what they said to each other. There is no communicative purpose. The only purpose of the open-ended question is to practise the language.

# How to Develop an Effective Writing Task?

Communication in writing is not a one-way process as there is someone expected to understand the message or the intent of the message we are trying to convey in writing. Writing to our doctor is not the same as writing to our brother, and therefore the context and purpose would dictate the way we write a message.

> **In a Nutshell …**
>
> The purpose of writing is not simply to practice language!

The purpose is the 'driver' of communication as we don't use language without a specific reason (e.g. write a list for groceries, leave a note to a friend, write a report or a letter). We write a grocery list with a specific purpose which is to buy some food and not simply to practise the language. Based on the view that an important aspect of L2 development is communication (although communication cannot be equated to language), the teaching of how we should develop language writing has changed.

> **In a Nutshell …**
>
> Communication in writing is not a one-way process as there is someone expected to understand the message or the intent of the message we are trying to convey.

The so-called product-oriented approach has been substituted by a more process-oriented approach where the focus is the development of a text rather than simply focusing on the production of a text. In real life, we write e-mails, notes, letters, grocery lists, reports, essays, and all these different tasks have a communicative purpose and a specific audience.

A process-oriented approach focuses on the creation of a text rather than concentrating only on the final product. A process-oriented approach takes into consideration the nature and role of communication and the cognitive processes involved in the development of competence in language writing.

> **In a Nutshell ...**
>
> In a process-oriented approach, the focus is the development of a text rather than simply focusing on the production of a text.

Developing the competence to write is somewhat neglected in L2 teaching, and very often, language teachers struggle to develop learners' effective language competence when it comes to writing. Teachers need to ensure that communication is at the heart of the language-written task to engage learners in meaningful and communicative language writing practice.

In developing the competence to write in the target language, learners are taught how to express their thoughts in a meaningful and appropriate way. The process of writing consists of two main sub-processes:

1. exploring specific themes or topics
2. set up specific objectives

Through writing, language learners can communicate information to a wider audience. Written tasks must promote communication, and at the same time facilitate language development.

> **Reflect on This ...**
>
> Do written tasks normally promote L2 development?

In analysing the role of writing in L2 development, two positions need to be distinguished: (1) the learning to write position and (2) the writing to learn the position.

The first position argues that developing writing competence is complex and it is only when L2 learners are already at an advanced language development stage that specific writing skills can be learned and taught. This approach equates competence in language writing to the achievement of some specific language objectives (e.g. the ability to write a formal and polite letter). Language teachers must first teach learners how to use language in a formal and polite context, for example.

> **In a Nutshell ...**
>
> Two positions in relation to the role of writing in L2 development:
>
> - the learning to write position and
> - the writing to learn position.

In the case of the second position, writing is considered as a vehicle for language development. A distinction is made between language writing as a basic exercise to learn content and language writing as a process conducive to language development. A typical example is for language teachers to set up a language task for learners where they need to use language in real-life contexts and purposes. In this case, the 'task' and not the 'specific objectives' is the main goal of the written activity. Another example is the so-called free writing activity where learners are asked by the teachers to write about a topic without worrying too much about the accuracy or appropriate use of language. Language teachers usually scaffold these activities giving learners some vocabulary and phrases to use. Learners have time to plan and interact with language using vocabulary and specific forms to complete their writing tasks.

In the context of the writing-to-learn position, theory and empirical research have investigated the role of written output in L2 development. Output is considered one of the elements of language development and it can be defined as the language learners produce in written or spoken forms to convey a specific message. Most perspectives in instructed L2 learning research do not hold that communicatively embedded output is a key element in L2 development.

> **In a Nutshell ...**
>
> Output might not affect language development, but it can facilitate the development of language writing skills.

However, there is clear support for the view that output can facilitate the development of language skills. Skill can be defined as the ability of learners to use language accurately and fluently. The so-called pushed output refers to speech or writing that encourages learners to express meaning through language production which must be accurate and appropriate. This is not the case with activities such as sentence dictation or drill practice which are meaningless and do not provide learners access to discourse.

Language learners move from input processing to ensure accurate interpretation of language to output processing needed for language production.

> ## What the Research Is Telling Us ...
> 
> Fact 1: Output might help learners to improve accuracy and fluency.
> 
> Fact 2: Output might help learners to notice a gap.

The written output might help learners to consolidate and to modify their accuracy and fluency. A possible beneficial function for output is to help learners notice existing gaps in their language knowledge. Output can be seen as an opportunity for learners to 'notice' the gap between what they want to say and what they can say. As they are trying to communicate something, they might become more aware of what they still need to learn about the target language and become more receptive to certain structures/forms. Written production might draw learners' attention to the form and structures they need to learn. Existing empirical evidence seems to suggest that output may facilitate the acquisition of certain features (e.g. words and verb inflections). However, current empirical evidence has not demonstrated that output assists in the development of syntax (word order).

> ## What the Research Is Telling Us ...
> 
> Fact 1: Output as part of interaction might have a facilitative role in language learning. It might facilitate the learning of words and their meanings.
> 
> Fact 2: No evidence to link output with the development of language competence in terms of mental representation of language (see Chapter 2). Mental representation refers to the formal properties of the language such as words, verbs, order of words in a sentence and so on.

> **In a Nutshell ...**
>
> Written language tasks should not engage learners in mechanical output practice where the language produced is meaningless.
>
> Written language tasks should be designed to facilitate language development by engaging learners in meaningful language production.

The need to develop writing competence should not mean that learners are engaged in mechanical output practice (e.g. drills, repetition exercises) where the language produced is meaningless. Written language tasks should be designed to facilitate language development by engaging learners in meaningful language production. In this context, a pedagogical intervention called a *structured output task* is a clear alternative to language mechanical drills. Structured output tasks have two components: (1) exchanging new information and (2) requiring L2 learners to access language (e.g. a form or structure) to process meaning (see Chapter 6).

In current language textbooks written activities focus on the production of grammatical and lexical structures (see example below). Language learners are provided with a list of words that they must use to write a short paragraph. Learners' practice is reduced to producing a text using grammar and words. The focus of the below activity is only to produce a text that contains particular words and grammatical items. In this practice, writing processes are minimum as the content is not as important as the use of the specific items. Planning will consist of constructing and ordering individual sentences. Reviewing will focus on which items in the list were used. Process-oriented approaches have shifted the focus on the audience and the purpose of writing engaging learners in authentic and interactive writing activities.

> Write a story/composition about how can young people spend their winter vacation in Italy using the elements in the three columns as a guide.
>
> | happy  | hotel | visit        |
> |--------|-------|--------------|
> | soon   | House | coming       |
> | always | Lake  | booked       |
> | hardly | You   | mountaineers |

| nice | mountain | travel |
| together | culture | found |
| difficult | holiday | sport |

# An Interactive Approach to Writing

Language teachers should design writing tasks to make learners produce a text for a communicative and meaningful purpose (e.g. writing an email to a friend, producing a poster for a company and the like). As argued earlier, traditional writing practice is often reduced to practising grammar or vocabulary that has just been learned.

> **In a Nutshell …**
>
> Traditional writing practice is often reduced to practice structures or vocabulary that it has just been learned (product-based approach).

The role of writing in the language classroom should involve creating content and tailoring this content to writers' needs. Language writing consists of an interaction of a variety of language processes, and learners possess specific strategies to deal with writing. Before starting to write, learners must define what we call 'the rhetorical problem'. What are the rhetorical problem's main elements?

1. the main purpose of the written text;
2. the main recipient/s of the written text;
3. the main topic of the written text;
4. learner's knowledge about the specific topic

Language learners should plan their writing very carefully. A processing approach to writing involves three main steps: (1) planning the composition, (2) generating ideas and (3) organizing ideas and setting goals.

> **In a Nutshell …**
>
> A processing approach to writing involves several steps:
>
> - planning the composition
> - generating ideas
> - organizing ideas and setting goals

This description of the processes involved in writing tells us how dynamic and complex writing is, regardless of whether the learner writes in his/her mother tongue or other languages. First of all, writing has a role in helping learners to acquire the target language. Language teachers might design writing activities to make learners learn new vocabulary for example. Secondly, writing can be used to produce a text for a specific purpose in a specific real-life context (e.g. writing an email, jotting a list of groceries or producing a poster). The role of writing should involve creating content and tailoring this content to writers' needs. When language learners are engaged in written tasks, they should plan the writing very carefully. Planning writing should involve several sub-processes: (1) exploring and deciding on the main ideas to convey in the composition, (2) planning how to present the ideas and (3) setting specific goals.

> **In a Nutshell ...**
>
> Traditional language writing practice is about producing structures or vocabulary that has just been learned. Practice is reduced to a matter of translating preconceived ideas into a text.

As outlined earlier, in traditional teaching, writing practice has focused on the texts that writers produce. In doing so, writing is simply reduced to a matter of translating preconceived ideas into a text. In existing language textbooks, written activities often focus on the production of grammatical and lexical forms. L2 learners are provided with a list of words that they must use to write a short paragraph or a series of sentences.

> **Reflect on This ...**
>
> What do we need to do as language teachers to make writing more interactive and effective in the language classroom?

Developing writing is a key component in developing learners' competence to communicate in a second language. Process-oriented approaches have shifted the focus on the audience and the purpose of writing. Using communicative composing-oriented written tasks that engage learners in authentic and interactive writing activities is what language instructors should consider. These types of tasks aim at improving learners' competence in writing and consist of three main phases: (1) the pre-writing phase, (2) the writing phase and (3) the focus on the language phase.

As teachers develop a writing task, they should initially consider the following: the familiarity of the subject chosen in the task, the overall purpose and authenticity of the task and the use of a stage-by-stage approach.

In an interactive writing task, a three-stage approach is proposed: pre-writing, writing and language focus. This approach would improve learners' writing competence as they will become better at coherently formulating their ideas and using correct syntax, grammar and vocabulary.

> **In a Nutshell ...**
>
> Interactive written tasks consist of three main stages:
> - pre-writing stage,
> - writing stage and
> - focus on the language stage.

- The pre-writing stage is the stage when language learners make decisions about the purpose of their composition.
- The writing stage is the stage when language learners achieve their plans to write a composition and meet the main objectives of the composition.
- The language focus stage is the stage when language learners have the opportunity to reflect on the content and aims of their composition and the language they have used to convey their message.

# The Pre-Writing Stage

This is the stage where language teachers facilitate the brainstorming of ideas about the composition and the nature of their writing task. Language learners have the opportunity to work in pairs or a group and jot down the main ideas. The teacher might use papers, pictures, and recordings to stimulate the discussion about a specific topic. The language teacher can also elicit appropriate vocabulary or phrases which students might find useful. During this stage, language learners also begin drafting the main ideas (skeleton) of their composition. At this stage, there should be no concerns about language accuracy.

## The Writing Stage

This is the stage where the language teacher acts simply as a classroom language facilitator and ensures that learners are linguistically supported in their composition. At this stage, language learners have made decisions about the audience and the main purpose of their composition. This stage comprises three main phases: (1) the task phase, (2) the planning phase and (3) the report phase.

(1) The task phase requires the language learners to begin to write about a specific purpose without concerns about the accuracy of the language used in terms of vocabulary and forms. The main focus of this phase is to get the message across in a meaningful way. (2) The planning phase instead requires both the language learner and the teacher to work together in an attempt to improve the overall correctness of the composition. (3) The report phase requires the language teacher to provide feedback and comments to the language learner about the written text.

## Language Focus Stage

This is the final stage of the writing task where the language learners would have a closer look at some of the specific features in the written composition. By this time, language learners have already used specific language to express meaning in the text, so they are ready to concentrate more closely on the formal properties of the language.

The example below (Figure 7.2) makes use of the pre-writing stage, the writing stage and the focus on language stage.

---

**Task:** Design a writing task using the three-phase approach:
Pre-writing stage:

Writing stage:

Focus on language stage:

---

**Figure 7.2** Written language task.
---
Pre-writing stage

Step 1. Working in a group of three you will have ten minutes to write up some ideas about whether or not and why our society is racist.

Step 2. Each group will present the ideas and a common list is agreed upon.

Step 3. Each student now will decide who will be the audience and the main purpose of the writing.

Writing stage

Step 1. Each student now needs to think about what to say and would need to prepare a summary of the composition which she/he then presents to the others in the group. This is an opportunity to verify content and exchange or add additional ideas.

Step 2. Each student will now need to write the text to the selected audience. He/she would need to check two things: (1) content and (2) organization.

- Content: Are the ideas you have included still the ones you want to have in the composition?
- Organization: Does the order in which the ideas are presented help convey the message to the selected audience?

If you answered 'no' to any question, rewrite some parts of the text.

Language focus stage

Step 1. When you consider your essay to be good enough, review the language you used:

   - Verbs: are forms, spelling and accent correct?
   - Adjectives: what noun do they go with? Are they appropriate?
   - Other elements of language you want your learners to focus on.
---

# Free-Writing Activity

Free-writing activities have the main purpose to get language learners to write down their ideas without worrying too much about accuracy. In the example below, learners are asked to write about the life of Albert Einstein.

# Free-Writing Task: The Life of Albert Einstein

Write down as much as you can about what you know of the life of this famous scientist. Do not worry about whether or not the content of your writing is accurate. Write without stopping and do not worry about accuracy. (Please note a short timeline about Albert's life).

**1887 Born in Germany > 1903 Married > 1905 Paper on the relativity theory > 1911 Full professor > 1921 Nobel Prize > 1933 Moved to USA 1939 > Manhattan project in USA > 1955 death**

The advantages of this approach are (1) providing language learners the opportunity to use language meaningfully, (2) producing language without paying too much attention to the structure of the language and (3) providing opportunities for learners to use the language and planning in writing before they need to use the language to develop other skills such as speaking.

> **Quiz:** Take the following short quiz to see what you have learned since the last quiz. You can circle more than one option.
>
> 1. A composing-oriented approach refers to ...
>    a. Written production task to practice grammar
>    b. Written production task to develop written competence
>    c. Written production task to practice vocabulary
>
> 2. A written interactive task is used to ...
>    a. Develop fluency
>    b. Develop accuracy
>    c. Develop the ability to communicate in writing

# Collaborative Writing

Empirical research investigating collaborative writing has demonstrated that it is an effective approach to language writing. It is effective in a variety of ways: (1) it stimulates reflective thinking, (2) it helps learners to focus on grammatical accuracy, lexis and discourse and (3) it encourages the development of knowledge about the language. Writing collaboratively might help language learners to notice gaps in their L2 production and then to test new hypotheses regarding the language. Further, learning is not seen just as the product of one individual's efforts, but as deeply connected to the surroundings, tools and the overall context in which the learning takes place. A typical example of collaborative writing is a dictogloss task.

Dictogloss is a type of task-based collaborative output that aims at helping learners to use their grammar resources to reconstruct a text and become aware of their shortcomings and needs. It consists of a listening phase and a reconstruction phase where learners are asked to reconstruct a text rather than write down the exact words that are dictated. As the text is read at a natural speed, students cannot write down every word but only keywords, and they have to understand the meaning and use their knowledge of grammar to reconstruct it.

The dictogloss procedure consists of four stages: (1) Preparation: when learners are informed about the topic of the text, and through a series of warm-up discussions, they are given the necessary vocabulary to cope with the task. It is at this stage that they are also organized into groups, (2) Dictation: when learners hear the text for the first time at natural speed. The first time they do not take any notes. The second time, language learners are asked to note down keywords to help them remember the content and reconstruct the text (3) Reconstruction: when learners work together in small groups and they need to reconstruct the text with correct grammar and content, (4) Analysis and Correction: when L2 learners analyse, compare and correct their texts. This is achieved with the help of the teacher and the other groups. Dictogloss is a very effective type of collaborative written task for several reasons: learners are encouraged to focus their attention on form and meaning and all four language skills are practised; learners develop a need for communication and group work; learners can monitor and adjust their interlanguage; learners have ample opportunity for discussion and negotiation.

## Takeaways from This Chapter

- Input is the main ingredient in language learning and plays an essential role.
- The role of output in L2 learning relates to the concept of skill and pushed output (speech or writing that demands learners to produce language correctly and appropriately).

- Written production can be linked to the development of the writing skill and the development of the lexicon and surface features of the language. There is no evidence that it can lead to the development of language as a system of mental representation.
- Possible roles for written output are:
  - Developing accuracy and fluency skills
  - Noticing. Language learners have the opportunity to notice a gap in their linguistic ability
  - Reflecting consciously on the linguistic features of the target language
  - Generating input for somebody else
- Process-oriented approaches have shifted the focus on the audience and the purpose of writing and engaging learners in authentic and interactive writing activities. This new approach has emphasized the importance of designing writing tasks that focus on meaning.
- A task is designed to increase successful learning and expose learners to meaningful input.
- A written task should have a clear set of procedures, and it can be monitored and evaluated by the teacher.
- Developing writing is a key component in developing learners' ability to communicate in a second language. Communicative composing-oriented tasks can enhance writing skills and provide learners with various options about the content of what they can write.
- The task-based approach proposed in this chapter considers the various cognitive processes and principles responsible for developing writing skills.
  - Defining the rhetorical problem (goal/purpose and audience);
  - Planning (generating ideas, organizing them, setting goals);
  - Reviewing (evaluation and review).
- Using communicative composing-oriented written tasks that engage learners in authentic and interactive writing activities is desirable. These types of tasks aim at improving learners' writing skills and consist of consists three phases:
- Pre-writing phase
- Writing phase
- Focus on the language phase
- Free writing tasks provide learners with the opportunity to use language meaningfully, to produce language without paying too much attention to the structure of the language and to use the

language and planning in writing before they need to use the language to develop other skills such as speaking.
- Collaborative writing can also be an effective approach to language writing. It is effective in a variety of ways: (1) it stimulates reflective thinking, (2) it helps learners to focus on grammatical accuracy, lexis and discourse and (3) it encourages the development of knowledge about the target language.

# Knowing More about the Subject

Benati, A. (2022). *Key terms for language teachers: A pocket guide*. Equinox.

Dave, W., & Willis, J. (2007). *Doing task-based teaching*. Oxford University Press.

DeKeyser, R. M. (2007). *Practice in a second language. Perspectives from applied linguistics and cognitive psychology*. Cambridge University Press.

Ellis, R. (2003). *Task-based language learning and teaching*. Oxford University Press.

Hyland, K. (2011). Learning to write: Issues in theory, research, and pedagogy. In R. M. Manchon (ed.), *Learning-to-write and writing-to-learn in an additional language* (pp. 17–35). John Benjamins.

Lee, J. (2000). *Tasks and communicating in language classrooms*, McGraw-Hill.

Lee, J., & VanPatten, B. (2003). *Making communicative teaching happen*. McGraw-Hill.

Long, M. (2015). *Second language acquisition and task-based language teaching*. Wiley Blackwell.

Long, M. H. (2016). In defence of tasks and TBLT: Non-issues and real issues. *Annual Review of Applied Linguistics, 36*, 5–33.

Long, M. H., Lee, J., & Hillman, K. (2019). Task-Based Language Learning. In J. Schwieter & A. Benati (eds), *The Cambridge handbook of language learning* (pp. 500–26). Cambridge University Press.

Polio, C. (2018). *Teaching second language writing*. Routledge.

Samuda, V., & Bygate, M. (2020). *Tasks in second language learning*. Palgrave.

Storch, N. (2002). Patterns of interaction in ESL pair work. *Language Learning, 52*: 119–58.

VanPatten, B., Smith, M., & Benati, A. (2019). *Key questions in second language acquisition: An introduction*. Cambridge University Press.

Williams, J. (2005). *Teaching writing in second and foreign language classrooms*. McGraw-Hill.

Wajnryb, R. (1990). *Grammar dictation*. Oxford University Press.

## Further Clarifications ...

In this section, we aim to further clarify some of the terms or concepts presented in the chapter.

**Skill** refers in this chapter to the ability to perform using language for speaking, listening, reading and writing. A skill involves the use of language to become accurate and fluent. It is juxtaposed with the concept of competence or mental representation of language.

**The task-based approach** is based on the idea that the use of 'language tasks' is the most effective way to teach and learn languages. This approach offers the opportunity for language learners to be exposed to communicative and meaningful classroom teaching. The language task is the main chapter, and the syllabus is organized by sequencing the pedagogical tasks.

# 8

# How Do We Teach Grammar and Correct Errors in the Language Classroom?

Overview 131
What Is the Role of Grammar Teaching in Language Learning? 132
How Do We Teach Grammar? 134
   Explanation of Grammar Rules 135
   Drills Practice 136
   Input-Based Focus on Form 139
   Output-Based Focus on Form 148
How Do We Choose What Type of Focus on Form to Use for Language Classroom Teaching? 152
How Do We Integrate Focus on Form in a Syllabus? 153
How Can We Assess the Effectiveness of Focus on Form in the Classroom? 154
How Do We Correct Errors? 156
   Elicitation 160
Knowing More about the Subject 163

## Overview

Language is a complex, abstract and implicit system. Language should not be taught like any other skill. This view has profound consequences for how we organize language teaching in the classroom. One of the key issues in second

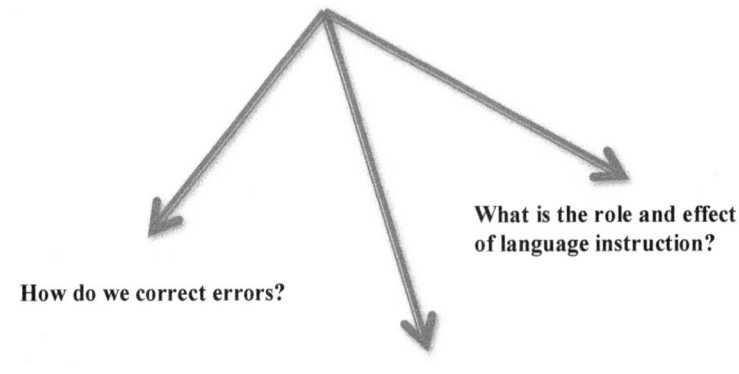

**Figure 8.1** Key questions of Chapter 8.

language instruction concerns the role and practice of grammar teaching. Does teaching grammar make a difference? Should we teach grammar? If so, how do we teach grammar in the language classroom?

These are some of the questions raised by scholars and teachers in search to find the most appropriate and effective way to introduce language learners to the grammar properties of a target language in the language classroom. The role and nature of corrective feedback will also be examined and discussed. In this chapter three main questions are addressed (Figure 8.1).

# What Is the Role of Grammar Teaching in Language Learning?

Language learners don't acquire one thing and then move on to another, as suggested by typical and traditional syllabi and textbooks. People's minds are constantly working on various aspects of the language simultaneously such that a little bit of one thing gets pencilled in while a little bit of something else also gets pencilled in the system. The language system develops over time and as highlighted in Chapter 1, language learning is stage-like and order-like. In the learning of any feature of the language, there are orders or stages of learning that all language learners go through regardless of their first language.

> ## What the Research Is Telling Us ...
>
> - Fact 1: Common developmental sequences have been observed for structures (e.g. negation, relative clauses, word order) in many languages.
> - Fact 2: Common orders of learning have been observed for forms (e.g. past -*ed*; pl – *s*) in many languages.
> - Fact 3: There are innate mechanisms that organize language in ways that can't be manipulated by practise.
> - Fact 4: Input is the basic ingredient in language learning. Our language system develops based on the input we can process.

One of the key issues in classroom language teaching concerns the role and practice of grammar. Does grammar teaching make a difference? Should we teach grammar? If so, how do we teach grammar in the language classroom? Is there an effective pedagogical intervention to teach grammar

> ## In a Nutshell ...
>
> - Grammar teaching does not affect the order of learning.
> - Grammar teaching does not affect the route of learning.
> - Grammar teaching might be beneficial to speed up learning.

that is better than other interventions? These are some of the questions that researchers and language teachers have addressed in their attempt to find the most appropriate and effective way to teach grammar. While many scholars address some of these questions to develop a better understanding of how people learn grammar, language teachers are in search of the most effective way to approach the teaching of grammar in the language classroom.

Empirical research investigating the role of grammar teaching in language learning has indicated the need for a so-called focus on form. The question is how this focus should be provided. There has been a dramatic shift from traditional grammar teaching to a more communicative approach.

In a traditional approach to focus on form (called 'focus on forms'), grammar teaching consists mainly of learning forms and structures by explicitly learning the rules, memorizing and practising them via pattern drills practice and translating texts. In a more effective approach to grammar teaching, a focus on form is incorporated within an overall focus on communication.

> **Task:** Some language teachers have argued that drills have a role in language learning (at least a psychological role) in helping learners to become more confident about their learning of a second language. However, research has shown that drills have no real value in language teaching.
>
> What is your view? Is drill practice an effective pedagogical technique in language teaching?
>
> Please now read VanPatten, B., & Wong, W. (2003). The evidence is IN: Drills are OUT. *Foreign Language Annals*, *36*, 403–23, and summarize the main concepts of this paper.

# How Do We Teach Grammar?

Language learners normally expect to get presentations and explanations of grammar rules from language teachers. In traditional approaches to grammar teaching, language teachers explain grammar rules (see examples in Figures 8.2 and 8.3) and this explanation is followed by mechanical drill practice (see examples in Figures 8.4 and 8.5).

**Figure 8.2** Explicit explanation of grammar rules (English past tense).

We use the past tense to talk about:

- something that happened **once in the past**:

*I talked to Paul yesterday.*

*We went to Italy for our holidays.*

*They played tennis last Sunday.*

- something that happened **several times in the past**:

*When I was young, I played football for a professional team.*

- something **true for some time in the past**:

*I lived abroad for ten years.*

**Figure 8.3** Explicit explanation of grammar rules (French perfect tense).

|             | -er verbs parler | -ir verbs choisir | -re verbs vendre |
|-------------|------------------|-------------------|------------------|
| j'ai        | parlé            | Choisi            | vendu            |
| tu as       | parlé            | Choisi            | vendu            |
| il/elle/on a| parlé            | Choisi            | vendu            |
| nous avons  | parlé            | Choisi            | vendu            |
| vous avez   | parlé            | Choisi            | vendu            |
| ils/elles ont | parlé          | Choisi            | vendu            |

**Figure 8.4** Drill practice (English past tense).

Complete the sentences with the past tense of the verb in brackets

1. I _____(phone) my brother yesterday

2. I _____(travel) to London

3. They_____(visit) me in Paris

**Figure 8.5** Drill practice (French perfect tense).

Complete the sentence with the passé composé.

1. Hier, la femme _____(voir) le garçon.

2. Ce matin, le garçon _____(parler) avec sa mère.

# Explanation of Grammar Rules

Learn how to use the past simple to talk about the past, and do the exercises to practise using it. With most verbs, the past tense is formed by adding *-ed* to the verb stem:

| Base form | Past tense form |
|-----------|-----------------|
| Call      | Call-ed         |
| Walk      | Walk-ed         |
| Work      | Work-ed         |

But there are a lot of irregular past tense forms in English. Here are the most common irregular verbs in English, with their past tense forms,

| Base form | Past tense form |
|---|---|
| Go | Went |
| Have | Had |
| Be | Was |

The perfect tense is used to talk about something that happened in the past – an action that is finished.

You need two parts to form the perfect tense with avoir:
The present tense of avoir
The **past participle** of the main verb
To get the past participle of regular verbs used with avoir:
Verbs ending **-er** - take off -er and add -é, eg parlé (spoke)
Verbs ending **-ir** - take off -ir and add -i, eg choisi (chose)
Verbs ending **-re-take** off -re and add -u, eg vendu (sold)

# The Perfect Tense of Regular Verbs with avoir

## Drills Practice

Transform the sentences below following the pattern.

**Example**: I play tennis - I <u>played</u> tennis

1. I clean the room          I _____ the room

2. I wash my hair            I _____ my hair

3. I work all day            I _____ all-day

## Reflect on This ...

Let's imagine you are going to start a new chapter called 'What we did last night and what that says about us.' Your first task in class is to tell students the following: 'OK, Class. I'm going to tell you five things I did last night [write what last night means in the first language on the board]. Last night. Ready? I watched the news. I prepared dinner. I walked my dog. I drank a cocktail. I called my sister on the phone. OK. Let's see what you remember. Whom did I call on the phone? What did I drink? What did I watch on TV? Excellent good memory! OK. Look up here on the screen. [the same five activities are on the screen] OK. With someone next to you, I'm giving you two minutes to put these activities in the order in which I did them. Go ahead. One through five....' Also, imagine this is the first time learners are exposed to the past tense in the language you teach.

How much do you have to explain about the past tense before you launch into this?

Anything?

All of it?

Just a little bit?

As previously argued, traditional grammar teaching is characterized by explicit teaching about grammar which is followed by pattern and drill practices as shown above. In this type of mechanical practice, the meaning and the message are ignored and the practice of a grammatical structure is implemented in a decontextualized way. Below is a common scenario of how often language teachers deal with grammar rules in the language classroom.

> *'Today we are going to learn about present tense forms. Does anyone know what the present tense is, how is formed, and how we use it? (silence from everyone in the class) Well, the present tense in Italian is formed by ... (present the class with a table (called a paradigm) with the rule of the present tense in Italian). For example in this sentence we add/change ... (quizzical look from students) ... What is the first person present of the verb 'to go'? If I need to say 'Today I go to play tennis' how do you say this in Italian? (one student ventures an answer).*

To complete a pattern drill practice, it is not necessary to understand any language. The learner must know how to mechanically produce the target form and can ignore the meaning of the language they produce.

Mechanical drills are problematic in language learning for three main reasons:

- They don't provide language learners with comprehensible and meaningful language input.
- They don't provide language learners with the opportunity to make form-meaning connections during exposure to the language.
- They only allow language learners to practice a specific form/structure in a mechanical way in the hope that learners can master the rule and become very accurate in the use of that form or structure. We know from the findings that this is not the case. Mechanical practice does not lead to accuracy!

This traditional type of grammar teaching (explanation + drill practice) is called 'focus on forms' and refers to the explicit teaching of specific linguistic forms one at a time. In opposition to this traditional approach, the term 'focus on form' instead is characterized by any pedagogical intervention which draws learners' attention to the grammatical properties of the target language by providing a focus on meaning and a focus on form at the same time. Below there is a visual representation of both terms about our learning model. A focus on form type of pedagogical intervention to grammar teaching goes from input to output and it facilitates language learning! This is not the case for 'focus on forms'.

$$\text{Input} \rightarrow \text{Intake} \rightarrow \text{Language System} \rightarrow \text{Output}$$
$$\uparrow \qquad\qquad\qquad\qquad\qquad \uparrow$$
$$\text{Focus on Form} \qquad\qquad \text{Focus on Forms}$$

### In a Nutshell …

A traditional approach to grammar instruction is characterized by paradigmatic explanations and mechanical drills.

The idea that acquiring grammar can be simply achieved by learning about grammatical rules and practising those rules through very mechanical output practice has been challenged by many scholars in the field. Empirical findings seem to point to the fact that a focus on form approach might facilitate the rate (the speed at which we process and learn a form) of learning if it is provided in combination with a focus on meaning.

# Input-Based Focus on Form

As previously said, input plays an essential role in language learning. Considering the limited role of traditional grammar teaching, and the importance of incorporating a component of focus on form in communicative language teaching, language teachers should look at devising grammar tasks that, on one hand, enhance the form in the input, and on the other hand, provide learners with opportunities to focus on meaning in the classroom.

## Structured Input

Unlike traditional teaching, where the focus of instruction is on the manipulation of learners' output, structured input aims at changing the way the input is processed by learners. Language learners, no matter their first language, use two main unconscious strategies to select and process information when they need to cope with the language they are exposed to.

The first one consists of processing words before forms in a sentence. The result of the use of this processing strategy is that they fail to make connections between one form and its meaning at input level. For example, in the case of a sentence such as *Last night I watched a great film with my friend Anna*, learners tend to process the first item in the sentence (*Last night*) before the form *-ed* as in *played*. Both elements of the sentence express the same semantic information (the idea that the action is completed). Because language learners have limited processing resources, their minds rely on the first element in the sentence to process the meaning of the sentence. In this way, they skip the form and they don't make a form-meaning connection.

The second strategy utilized by language learners is when they process the first noun they encounter in a sentence as the subject of that sentence. For example, in a sentence such as *Jane was kissed by Paul*, learners would interpret the sentence as if it were Jane who kissed Paul. Misinterpreting the meaning inevitably causes a delay in learning this structure (passive construction).

Structured input activities aim at altering these two default processing strategies adopted by learners in their efforts to comprehend language. The main aim of structured input activities is to ensure language learners process input more effectively and make accurate form-meaning connections (e.g. connect *-ed* as in *played* to its full meaning = the action of *play* is completed). Structured input is a type of focus on the form which through input manipulations guides learners to focus on form to process meaning in language input. Specific guidelines have been designed for developing structured input activities:

1. Present one form at a time
2. Keep meaning in focus
3. Move from sentences to connected discourse
4. Use both oral and written input
5. Have the learner do something with the input
6. Keep the learner's processing strategies in mind

1. Language learners should be exposed to one form at a time. Teachers do not need to provide learners with explicit information about the form. The main reasons for exposing learners to one form at a time are (1) learners possess a limited capacity for processing and storing information in their working memory (this is a processing space where learners initially store information) and (ii) learners process and intake one form and one meaning at a time. Adopting this first guideline will enhance the opportunity for learners to intake language input and make the right form-meaning connections.

2. Keeping meaning in focus is crucial when we develop structured input activities. In structured input, learners must process the meaning of the input to complete the activity and make the correct connections with the form.

3. Learners are first exposed to sentences in the input before connected discourse. This should happen only when learners have already had opportunities to process the new form at the sentence level.

4. Structured input activities which combine oral and written input should be used. This is to account for the development of both listening and reading competence. Hearing the form would facilitate learners to make sound-meaning connections, whereas written form-meaning connections would be made via reading.

5. Structured input activities should be designed to make learners do something with the input they receive (i.e. agreeing or disagreeing; choosing options such as false or true; likely or unlikely). During structured input activities, learners should be encouraged to make form-meaning connections. Learners must engage in processing the input (having a specific reason for processing input) and must respond to the input sentence in some way.

6. Learners' processing should be guided so that learners do not rely on natural/universal processing strategies. Activities in which the input is structured to alter the learner's reliance on one particular processing strategy should be created. The main goal of structured input activities is correcting inefficient processing strategies and instilling in learners the ability to make appropriate form-meaning connections.

**Figure 8.6** Referential structured input activity.

1) John had his car washed last Monday
2) Jane had his hair cut
3) Marc had his house painted white

**Figure 8.7** Referential structured input activity.

1. ... jouait au football dans le monde entier
2. ... gagnait beaucoup de coupes.
3. ... passe du temps avec sa famille.
4. ... participait à beaucoup de diners officiels.
5. ... s'entrainait avec Ronaldo.
6. ... s'occupe de ses enfants.
7. ... est directeur de l'association ELA.
8. ... téléphone à Thierry Henri pour discuter.
9. ... marquait beaucoup de buts.
10. ... était le meilleur joueur de football au monde.

Structured input activities are of two types: referential (Figures 8.6 and 8.7), and affective (Figures 8.8 and 8.9). Referential activities are those for which there is a right or wrong answer and learners must rely on the form to get meaning. In the referential structured input example below, the input is structured in a way that learners need to rely on the form (causative structure) to correctly understand the meaning of the input they are exposed to. All sentences are meaningful and learners are asked to interpret input correctly.

Listen to the sentences and answer the questions. Pay careful attention to the structure of each sentence to understand **who** is acting.

| | | |
|---|---|---|
| Who washed the car? | (a) John | (b) someone else |
| Who cut the hair? | (a) Jane | (b) someone else |
| Who painted the house? | (a) Marc | (b) someone else |

**Figure 8.8** Affective structured input activity.

**Step 1.** Indicate which of the following things happened to you in real life. Be prepared to share with the class.

|  | Yes | No |
|---|---|---|
| 1. I had my vehicle repaired | ☐ | ☐ |
| 2. I had my hair cut | ☐ | ☐ |
| 3. I had my photo taken | ☐ | ☐ |
| 4. I had my bills paid | ☐ | ☐ |
| 5. I had my mobile phone stolen | ☐ | ☐ |

**Step 2.** As the instructor reads the statements, raise your hand if it is true for you. Someone should keep a record on the board.

**Step 3.** Let's find out now which are the three most popular and the three least popular things to do in our class.

**Figure 8.9** Affective structured input activity.

**Step 1.** Indicate whether or not you agree or disagree with each of the predictions listed below. Some of this will probably happen in the next ten years. Compare your response with someone else.

|  | Sono d'accordo | Non sono d'accordo |
|---|---|---|
| 1. una donna diventerà presidente degli USA | ☐ | ☐ |
| 2. si troverà il vaccino per l'AIDS | ☐ | ☐ |
| 3. l'Italiano diventerà la lingua più importante d' Europa | ☐ | ☐ |
| 4. l'uomo arriverà sul pianeta Marte | ☐ | ☐ |
| 5. il Galles diventerà uno stato indipendente | ☐ | ☐ |
| 6. l'Irlanda del Nord diventerà una repubblica | ☐ | ☐ |
| 7. il Papa muorirà | ☐ | ☐ |
| 8. si troverà il vaccino per il cancro | ☐ | ☐ |
| 9. si sconfiggerà il terrorismo | ☐ | ☐ |
| 10. scoppierà la terza guerra mondiale | ☐ | ☐ |

**Step 2.** Confront your answer with your partner. Sei ' pessimista' o 'ottimista'?

☐ ☐

Teaching Grammar and Correcting Errors    143

# Instructor's Script

Listen to the following statements made by a journalist about the life of Zinédine Zidane and decide whether each statement is referring to his past life as a professional football player or his life now as a retired football player.

| Professional football player | Retired football player |
|---|---|
| ☐ | ☐ |
| ☐ | ☐ |
| ☐ | ☐ |
| ☐ | ☐ |
| ☐ | ☐ |
| ☐ | ☐ |
| ☐ | ☐ |
| ☐ | ☐ |

# Sentences Heard

Zinédine Zidane...

In the affective structure input activity below, learners are asked to interpret the sentences containing English causative forms and then undertake several other steps afterward.

The advantage of the use of structured input is twofold: (1) it is an effective pedagogical intervention at altering processing strategies learners take to the task of comprehension of language in

### In a Nutshell ...

Structured input activities aim at altering processing strategies learners take to the task of comprehension and to encourage them to make better form-meaning connections.

the input; (2) it is a pedagogical intervention that through the manipulation and restructuring of the input help language learners to acquire one form at a time by making correct and appropriate form-meaning connections.

## Textual Enhancement and Input Flood

Language learners must be exposed to input and that input must be comprehensible and convey a message to speed up learning. Learners need to notice and process (making an appropriate form-meaning connection) a form in the input. Given the importance of 'notice a form' in the input, our questions are: What is noticing? How can we best facilitate the noticing of a certain form in the input?

Noticing is becoming aware of the properties of a language in the input, and it requires attention from the language learner. Noticing is different from processing which requires learners to make a connection between the form and its meaning. To learn a language, input data must be processed (linked to meaning) during comprehension (e.g. a past tense marker such as *-ed* has to be tagged as meaning <+past> <-present> for the language to be acquired).

> ### Consider This ...
> Noticing means that learners are aware of something. This is in contrast with learning which involves subconscious processes. Being aware of something does not mean that 'that something' has been implicitly processed and acquired. Please refer to Chapter 1 and the discussion around roles of explicit and explicit in L2 learning.

Input enhancement is a type of grammar teaching which enhances the input to facilitate language learners in noticing a specific form in the input. The enhancement should affect learners' ability to notice the form in the input. Various ways of enhancing the input have been proposed which differ in terms of explicitness and elaboration. A practical example would be to underline or capitalize a specific form in a text to help learners notice that particular form (textual enhancement). A different pedagogical intervention would be to modify a text so that a particular target item would appear over and over again so that the text will contain many more exemplars of the same feature (input flood).

In textual enhancement, a form is made more noticeable to the learner. To help learners notice a particular feature, the language teacher should provide learners with typographical cues such as bolding the form to draw their attention to it in the text. Textual enhancement is used to make particular features of language input more salient with the scope to help learners notice them and eventually make accurate form-meaning connections. The target form is enhanced by visually altering (see activity in Figure 8.10) its appearance in the text (italicized, bolded, underlined). Oral input enhancement can also be provided by using special stress, intonation, and gestures in spoken input.

> **In a Nutshell ...**
>
> Input enhancement is a pedagogical intervention that enhances the input to allow learners to notice some specific forms in the input.
>
> Textual enhancement and input flood are two different ways of enhancing and manipulating input to focus on form.

Designing textual enhancement activities will involve following these guidelines:

1. Choose a grammatical form that learners need to pay attention to. There are 'forms' that language learners would find difficult to learn because of the lack of frequency in the input not being noticeable and redundant, for example (another element in the sentence expressing the same meaning);
2. Highlight the feature in the text using a textual enhancement technique (e.g. bolding, underlying). This is a technique to increase the saliency of this form in the input so as to increase opportunities for noticing;
3. Keep the learner's attention on meaning. Again, the main objective is to enhance the opportunities to make form-meaning connections;
4. Do not provide any explanation about the form.

The main advantages of textual enhancement are threefold: (1) language learners are exposed to enhanced and manipulated language input where they have the opportunity to notice the target form; (2) learners will be exposed to meaning-bearing input from this type of tasks; (3) it is a form of input enhancement that can be easily integrated and it is easy to use.

**Figure 8.10** Textual enhancement activity.

**Step 1. Please read this text carefully. You will be asked to complete comprehension activities after you have read the text.**

Alessandro **works** at the University of Dublin where he is a professor of linguistics. He **goes** to university every day and he always take**s** the car. Every Saturday, Alessandro **watches** football with his friends. On Sunday, he **plays** tennis in the park and **visits** the university gym for some exercise. He **loves** cooking Italian food and … (The text continues).

**Step 2. Please circle the correct answer for each question based on the information you read about Alessandro.**

What sports does he play?

| Tennis | Football | Basketball |
|---|---|---|
| ☐ | ☐ | ☐ |

How does it go to work?

| Car | Bus | Train |
|---|---|---|
| ☐ | ☐ | ☐ |

(The task continues similarly)

**Step 3. Guess whether the statements about your professor are true (T) or false (V).**

|  | T | V |
|---|---|---|
| Your professor **loves** cooking | ☐ | ☐ |
| Your professor **loves** playing tennis. | ☐ | ☐ |
| Your professor **likes** the gym | ☐ | ☐ |
| Your professor **drives** a car | ☐ | ☐ |
| (The activity continues similarly) | ☐ | ☐ |

---

**Task:** Can you develop a structured input and a textual enhancement activity following the guidelines provided?

## Input Flood

Input flood is an implicit type of focus on form. In input flood, the input learners receive is saturated with the form that we hope learners might notice and possibly acquire. The form is not highlighted in any way. When designing input flood activities the following guidelines should be followed:

1. Activities using input flood should either be used in written or oral input;
2. The input learners receive must be modified so that it contains many instances of the same form or structure. This is to provide language learners with ample opportunities to encounter a certain form (increase frequency in the input). Learners are likely to notice the form and the meaning of the form without any grammatical explanations or error corrections;
3. Input flood must be meaningful and learners must be doing something with the input (i.e. reconstruct a story, draw a picture, answer content questions) they are exposed to.

The main purpose of designing input flood activities (see an input flood activity in Figure 8.11) is to help language learners be exposed to a greater amount of input containing the target form (past tense in English is flooded in the example below) which should allow learners to notice and subsequently acquire this form. Overall, advantages of input flood

**Figure 8.11** Input flood activity.

Last Saturday, Richard jumped out of bed at 8.00 am. He poured himself 3 strong cups of coffee to wake up fully. He watched TV and slowly felt more awake. He wanted to go back to sleep again, but he remembered that he had worked on Saturdays. He worked part-time at Starbucks café and the manager was very strict. He walked quickly to the bus stop, but unfortunately, there was a lot of traffic and so he waited for over an hour. He eventually arrived late and his manager was extremely angry. He shouted at him and said he was a useless employee. Things got worse when Richard spilled a customer's coffee all over the floor and his boss got angry and informed him that he was sacked. Finally, Richard returned home feeling miserable and exhausted. What a horrible Saturday. At least he could sleep in on Sunday!

(Text continues)

Follow-up: After you hear the text, in pairs, give as many details as you can remember about Richard's horrible day. The group with the most details wins. You have three minutes.

are: (1) input flood material can be accommodated easily to any subject in which learners are interested; (2) the teacher can simply manipulate any materials so that this input contains many uses of a particular target form.

> **Reflect on This ...**
>
> Explain why you might agree or do not agree with the following statement:
>
> 'Because teaching grammar does not affect the order we learn grammar, there is no need to worry about teaching grammar.'

## Output-Based Focus on Form

Input is necessary for language learning, but it might not be enough for developing the ability of learners to use language to express meaning. Language learners need opportunities to express a particular meaning by retrieving a particular form (the ability to string forms together) from their language system. The fact that learners incorporate forms in the language system through form-meaning connections, and the system grows gradually like a 'web of connections', does not mean that learners can automatically access language for speech production.

Despite the role that output might then play in language learning, mechanical output practice (see Figure 8.12) *does not* help learners to access the necessary information in the language system necessary for meaningful production.

**Figure 8.12** Mechanical output practice.

Use the following verbs to describe what you have done this weekend.

Model: play ➜ I *have played*

1. study

2. sleep

3. watch TV

Structured output activities are an effective alternative to mechanical output practice. Ineffective output focus on form activities; language learners must understand the meaning of both the stimulus and their answer. The range of learner responses must be open and no single correct response exists. Structured output activities have two main characteristics:

- They involve the exchange of previously unknown information;
- They require learners to access a particular form or structure to process meaning.

To develop structured output tasks the following guidelines should be followed:

1. Present one thing at a time (one form/one function)
2. Keep meaning in focus (obtaining information)
3. Move from sentences to connected discourse (string sentences together)
4. Use both oral and written output (prepare questions and interview somebody)
5. Others must respond to the content of the output (the output created contains a message and someone must respond to the content of the message, e.g. comparing, taking notes, filling out a grid or chart, signing something, indicating agreement, responding)
6. The learner must have some knowledge of the form or structure (should follow structured input tasks)

In the example below (Figure 8.13) the focus is on one form and one meaning and learners have to respond to the content of the output.

> **Reflect on This ...**
>
> What do you think about the role of output?
>
> How can we develop effective output grammar practice for the language classroom?

> **Task:** Can you design a structured output activity following the guidelines provided?

**Figure 8.13** Structured output activity.

**Step 1.** Indicate which of the following activities you did **yourself** and which **you asked someone else** to do for you last week.

***Example***: 'I tidied my room last week but I had my desk dusted by my brother because I'm allergic to dust.'

| Chores | Done by myself | Have it done by someone else |
|---|---|---|
| Clean the windows | | |
| Mop the floor | | |
| Do the dishes | | |
| Cook dinner | | |
| Iron the clothes | | |
| Repair something | | |
| Do the laundry | | |

**Step 2.** Using the information from step 1, create a series of questions (maximum 5) to ask your classmate during an interview.

***Example***: 'Did you tidy your room yourself or did you have it tidied by someone else last week?'

**Step 3.** Interview your classmate. Be sure to write down your classmate's responses because you will need them later.

**Step 4.** Prepare a set of statements (maximum 5) in which you compare the chores you ask someone else to do for you with the chores your classmate asks someone else to do for him/her using the ideas from steps 1, 2 and 3. You will present your results to the class and after you have received feedback from other classmates you will draw some conclusions about which chores are the least popular among the students of your class.

## What the Research Is Telling Us ...

Fact 1: Structured input is an effective focus on form at helping language learners to make accurate form-meaning connections. This is the case for a form or structure affected by processing problems.

Fact 2: Textual enhancement is an effective focus on form at helping language learners to notice a form or structure in the input. The effectiveness of this type of focus on form depends on the proficiency level of language learners, the developmental stage and the degree of readiness of the learner, the type of form chosen and the intensity of the treatment.

Fact 3: Input flood is an effective focus on form at helping language learners to notice a form or structure in the input. The effectiveness of this type of focus on form depends on the length of the treatment and the nature of the linguistic feature.

As we have previously said, traditional grammar teaching is not an appropriate way to approach grammar instruction. The grammatical explanation of a rule followed by mechanical and meaningful drill practice is not an effective way to focus on form in the language classroom.

However, there are pedagogical interventions to grammar teaching which, as described in this chapter, are in certain cases and conditions, effective ways to incorporate a focus on form in a communicative and meaningful approach to language teaching.

### In a Nutshell ...

Structured output activities have two main characteristics:

- They involve the exchange of previously unknown information;
- They require learners to access a particular form or structure in order to process meaning.

### Reflect on This ...

Why is it important for learners to attend to meaning in output practice?

Can you underscore the difference between structured input and structured output activities?

**Quiz** Take the following short quiz to see what you have learned in this module. Circle a, b or c Answers are provided at the end.

1. Explicit information ...

    a. Might help speed up language learning

b. Changes the route of language learning
   c. It is not effective

2. A focus on form intervention that involves manipulating typographical cues is …

   a. Textual enhancement
   b. Structured input
   c. Structured output

3. A type of focus on form that involves restructuring input grammatically is …

   a. Input flood
   b. Input enhancement
   c. Structured input

4. Grammar should be taught mechanically.

   a. True
   b. False
   c. Not true and not false

5. Which of the following does not describe structured input?

   a. Referential and affective activities
   b. Practice after explanation of rules
   c. The output that it elicits is always meaningful

# How Do We Choose What Type of Focus on Form to Use for Language Classroom Teaching?

The effects of different types of 'focus on form' have been investigated in classroom settings. Overall, the results indicate that input-based options of focus on the form might have a facilitative role in speeding up the rate of learning of certain grammar features. Despite this, in a classroom setting, teachers should not be limited to the use of one type of 'focus on form'. They can use many types of 'focus on form' at the same time during a lesson. They might use a structured input activity to ensure learners make an appropriate form-meaning connection and this can be followed by a textual enhancement activity to ensure learners can have additional chances to notice the same form and reinforce form-meaning connections.

In choosing a type of 'focus of form', teachers should also consider the nature of the target form. One of the criteria used to characterize a form is whether or not it is transparent. A transparent form has a distinct meaning that corresponds to it. For example, -*ing* morpheme in English has a clear form meaning relationship, that is, an action that is not completed in the present. Plural -*s*- in English has a transparent form-meaning relationship with a clear corresponding meaning distinction: -*s*- expresses plurality (*car* vs. *cars*). *May* or *might* are not transparent forms because they do not have a clear meaning distinction. They can express possibility, but they can also be used to express the idea of permission.

Input flood and textual enhancement will be more effective with transparent forms. During input enhancement, learners would need to make form-meaning connections based on the input alone. Therefore, the form will need to have a transparent form-meaning relationship, otherwise, learners might find it difficult to interpret the meaning that the form encodes, even if they notice the form (e.g. typographical cues increase perceptual salience of a form).

Structured input activities are a type of focus on the form which is suitable for a form with a less transparent form-meaning relationship. L2 learners must both notice and process the form to complete the activity. Structured input activities must be used if a form is particularly affected by a processing problem or a combination of problems. In the case of -*ed*- past tense regular forms in English, this form is affected by its position in the sentence and its redundancy which makes it difficult for learners to make accurate form-meaning connections.

In the sentence *Yesterday, I played tennis with Colin*, the -*ed*- in play is in the middle of the sentence (the first element usually processed first by learners) and is made redundant (express the same semantic meaning) by the temporal adverb (*Yesterday*). Language teachers need to consider the characteristic of the form to teach, to choose the most effective type of 'focus on form' approach.

# How Do We Integrate Focus on Form in a Syllabus?

The implicit nature of input flood and textual enhancement allows them to be integrated into all types of syllabi without interrupting the content of teaching. If language learners have difficulty with a particular form, teachers can flood the activity with the target form. Textual enhancement can also be easily integrated to increase the frequency and saliency of a form in an activity such as reading comprehension text. Structured input can be used to cover the learning of certain features (e.g. tenses, word order, passive constructions) in the syllabus affected by processing problems.

# How Can We Assess the Effectiveness of Focus on Form in the Classroom?

The textual enhancement type of 'focus on form' increases the chances for learners to pay attention to the target form. They should have a better chance to notice the form and hopefully process the meaning that the form encodes. However, there is no guarantee that a form-meaning connection is made. If we wish to assess whether input flood or textual enhancement is effective or not, we need to ensure we include activities that require learners to notice the target form. Completing a structured input activity is more of a guarantee that language learners have noticed the form and also processed its meaning. In structured input practice, learners have to process the form to get the meaning. In this sense, this practice is in itself, a way to assess noticing and the successful mapping of one form to one meaning.

> **Task:** Read the following study on the role of grammar instruction in language teaching and complete the grid below: Benati, A. (2020). The effects of structured input and traditional instruction on the acquisition of the English causative forms: An eye-tracking study measuring accuracy in responses and processing patterns. Language *Teaching Research*, *24*, 1–21.
>
> | Purpose |
> | --- |
> | Questions |
> | Design |
> | Results |
> | Interpretation |

| Implications |
| Limitations/future research |

## Takeaways from This Chapter

- Traditional grammar teaching is not an appropriate way to teach grammar. Explanation of a grammatical rule followed by mechanical and meaningful drill practice is not an effective way to focus on form in the language classroom. However, there are types of 'focus on form' that can in certain cases and conditions enhance and speed up the way grammar is acquired.
- Structured input activities help learners to process input correctly and efficiently and therefore increases learner's intake.
- Textual enhancement and input flood provide learners with access to comprehensible input and help learners to pay attention to the targeted form in the input.
- Structured output activities are useful as they provide learners with an opportunity to produce output for a specific and meaningful purpose.
- Here are some of the principles language teachers should take into consideration when developing grammar activities for teaching in the language classroom:
    1. Focus on form should be developed to ensure that learners process input correctly and efficiently;
    2. Focus on form should be designed for learners to notice and process forms in the input and eventually make appropriate correct form-meaning connections;
    3. Focus on form should include both a focus on form and a focus on meaning;
    4. Focus on form should move from input to output practice. Structured output activities should be used to engage learners in language production

Input → Intake → Language system → Output →

→ ↑

Textual Enhancement    Structured Output

    Input Flood

Structured input

> **Task:** Please provide a full answer to these three questions:
> 1. How do we move from input to output in grammar teaching?
> 2. Why do you think explicit information and drills practice are so entrenched in the mind of many language teachers?
> 3. Which of the input enhancement techniques or focus on form interventions do you see being able to use in the classroom? Why would you select this particular focus on form?

# How Do We Correct Errors?

One of the key questions for researchers and teachers is: Does error correction contribute to language learning? There are conflicting views around the role and nature of error correction which from now on we call 'corrective feedback'. From a theoretical perspective, three main views exist around the nature of corrective feedback: (1) the nativist view, (2) the interactionist view and (3) the cognitivist view. The point of departure for the nativist view is how L1 learning happens. There is a limited provision of corrective feedback in L1 learning as children acquire the language mainly through exposure to the language input they are abundantly exposed to. What drives language learning is some biologically innate linguistic principles called Universal Grammar that are accessible to all learners from the time they are born (see again Chapters 1 and 2). According to Universal Grammar, the learner's mind is so powerful that there is comparatively little that a language teacher can do. Thus, what language learners mainly need is exposure to the correct input, and corrective feedback hardly plays any role.

> ### Reflect on This ...
> Universal Grammar refers to the fact that humans are not little mimics who merely repeat what they hear around them. Humans are active creators of a linguistic system and are guided by innate knowledge. This innate structure consists of abstract linguistic principles we have in our mind/brain – principles such as all sentences must have subjects that have a structural relationship to verbs.

The interactionist view asserts that corrective feedback exists in interactions between parents and children in the L1 and it is an important source for L1 learners. Corrective feedback also takes place in L2 learning through interactions between the native speaker (NS) and the non-native speaker (NNS). As previously said, negotiation of meaning allows learners to interact with each other and this type of interaction plays a facilitative role in language learning as it attempts to remedy communication breakdown among interlocutors. The interactionist position recognizes the importance of comprehensible input and views interactional corrective feedback as an important factor in making input comprehensible (language that is easy to understand).

A cognitivist view sees language acquisition as driven by cognitive processes. Thus, corrective feedback might have a facilitative role in helping learners to develop a mental representation of the target language.

There are also conflicting pedagogical views around the role and nature of corrective feedback. From an audiolingual/behaviourism perspective, making an error is seen as a sin and should be immediately corrected before it becomes a bad habit. Corrective feedback is therefore essential for eradicating errors.

Contrary to this view, a more communicative approach to language teaching would assert that learners go through predetermined sequences of acquisition not much affected by instruction, and corrective feedback is unnecessary and even detrimental as it interrupts the natural learning process.

> **In a Nutshell …**
>
> Negotiation of meaning is when we engage with another speaker to clarify the message conveyed. Clarification requests such as 'what did you say?' help us to understand the meaning of an interaction between two speakers.

> **In a Nutshell …**
>
> - Nativist view = no role for corrective feedback
> - Interactionist view = beneficial role for corrective feedback
> - Cognitivist view = beneficial role for corrective feedback

Corrective feedback has the immediate effect of putting the learner on the defensive. It encourages a strategy in which the learner will try (1) to avoid mistakes, (2) to avoid difficult constructions and (3) focuses less on meaning and more on the form.

Classroom-based research has shown that it is possible to provide corrective feedback without interrupting the flow of communication, and this can be achieved by integrating the feedback into a meaningful interaction. Corrective feedback refers to feedback that learners receive on their erroneous or inappropriate utterances during (conversational) interaction. Corrective feedback is usually provided to the learner in two ways: positive evidence (provision of the correct form) and negative evidence (pointing out the error and providing a grammatical explanation).

Corrective feedback can be provided through various forms of negotiation strategies, such as recasts, clarification requests, confirmation checks and direct elicitation, which are generally used to deal with communication breakdown.

> **In a Nutshell ...**
>
> There are different types of corrective feedback:
>
> - Recasts
> - Clarification requests
> - Confirmation checks
> - Direct elicitation?

The input of one speaker is modified by another speaker and this is normally due to a lack of comprehension (e.g. What did you say? Do you mean *tonight*? Sorry?) and a communication breakdown. Corrective feedback between two interlocutors indicates that some of their output is not correct. Conversational interaction between NS and NNS might facilitate language learning (see the example below).

Teacher/NS: Where did you spend your holiday?
Student/NNS: I went in vacation to Italy (trigger)
Teacher/NS: Oh, you went *on* vacation to Italy? (feedback) wonderful
Student/NNS: Yup, I *went on* vacation in Tuscany (uptake)

> **Reflect on This ...**
>
> There are different types of corrective feedback. Which is the most effective one in your view? And why?

Classroom-based research has examined the effects of corrective feedback in classroom contexts. Two overall types of corrective feedback have been investigated: (1) reformulation and (2) elicitation.

Reformulation type of corrective feedback provides learners with the correct form immediately after their erroneous sentence. Elicitation refers to other corrective feedback interventions which do not provide learners with the correct form. Language learners are encouraged to repair their errors by providing them with a prompt and thus a chance to reformulate their utterances. An interactional modification such as a comprehension check or a request for clarification between two interlocutors (NS and NSS and/or NNS and NNS) during communication occurs through a process called 'negotiation of meaning'. Negotiation of meaning has two main roles: (1) helping learners to comprehend the message contained in the input and (2) facilitating the production of modified output after learners receive corrective feedback on their erroneous output.

## Recast

A reformulation type of correct feedback is called 'recast'. Recast by definition refers to a reformulation of learners' erroneous sentences into a correct form without sacrificing an overall focus on meaning. Recast is used by language teachers to make sure that the speaker becomes aware that something is wrong in their production (see examples below). The NS reformulates the whole or part of the learner's erroneous sentence into a correct form while maintaining the overall focus on meaning.

NNS: …this thing annoys me…
NS: Oh, why it annoys you?
NNS: It annoys me because it is unfair…
NS: Yea, I agree, you are right…

In the above example, the NNS produces a sentence that contains an error. The NS (instructor) reformulates the learner's incorrect form into a correct form. The successful correction made by the NNS is called uptake. The NS continues the interaction in an attempt not to break the flow of communication.

The line of research into the effects of corrective feedback has overall indicated that recast is a beneficial type of implicit error correction as it enables language learners to be exposed to the correct form without interrupting the flow of communication. Recast draws L2 learners' attention to their incorrect form and facilitates uptake through self-repair. Recast seems more effective with beginner learners as they find it more difficult to recognize their errors.

# Elicitation

An elicitation type of corrective feedback is called a 'clarification request'. It occurs when there is a breakdown of communication between two interlocutors (teacher and learner, NS and NNS). The teacher does not provide the learner with the correct form. However, it gives the learner the opportunity for self-repair. Phrases such as 'sorry?' or 'what did you say?' provide the learner with an opportunity to clarify and/or make his sentence/speech more accurate.

Metalinguistic feedback provides NNS with a metalinguistic cue in the input (see the example below). The feedback can include comments about grammatical rules and/or questions about the accuracy of learners' output. Metalinguistic feedback can be provided in the form of giving learners a clue and promoting self-repair.

NNS: I go to college yesterday.
NS: You need a past tense (metalinguistic cue)

> **In a Nutshell ...**
>
> There are two overall types of corrective feedback:
>
> - Reformulation;
> - Elicitation.

Direct elicitation is another type of corrective feedback used in an attempt to elicit the correct form. The teacher is repeating the learner's utterance up to the error. There is no correction but an opportunity for learners to self-repair (see the example below).

NNS: And when the young girl arrives, ah, besides the old woman.
NS: When the young girl …?

The role of corrective feedback has been investigated in instructed second learning research. This branch of research has attempted to demonstrate whether or not interactional feedback contributes to L2 learning, how it affects learning and what kind of feedback is the most effective.

A substantial body of research measuring the role and effects of corrective feedback is available. The empirical research into the effects of elicitation has overall indicated that it is beneficial as it allows opportunities for self-correction and pushes language learners to produce output. However, we should not assume that an immediate reaction in response to feedback provides a valid measure of language learning. Even when there is uptake, that uptake can be simply a mechanical repetition of the feedback. Elicitation seems more effective with advanced-level learners because they can recognize their errors.

> **Reflect on This ...**
>
> What are the advantages and disadvantages to use corrective feedback?

Corrective feedback might play a facilitative role in helping learners process linguistic items of the target language through the language input they receive. The information provided to learners through corrective feedback should allow them to confirm, falsify and/or modify the language they produced.

> **In a Nutshell ...**
>
> There are two types of uptake:
> - Uptake that produces a new sentence still needing repair
> - Uptake that produces a repair of the error on which the language instructor's feedback is focused

If we assume that errors should be corrected to provide opportunities for learners to develop their language competence, the question is: What form of corrective feedback is the most appropriate to facilitate learning? Although more classroom research is needed to answer fully this question, the empirical evidence so far on the role of corrective feedback seems to indicate that it might be more effective for learners when it is provided more implicitly and when learners are provided with opportunities to negotiate meaning.

Corrective feedback is more effective when learners are actively engaged in negotiating a form, or when they have to think about and respond to the language teacher's feedback in some way. The opportunity of negotiating forms is achieved in a better way when the language instructor does not provide the correct form, but instead, he/she provides cues in the input to help the learner consider how to reformulate his or her incorrect language. The effectiveness of corrective feedback might also be affected by developmental sequences. Learners acquire a form when they are developmentally ready.

Developmentally ready means that language learners traverse various stages in acquiring single structures of the language. For instance, the acquired 'negations' goes through stages where the negator is initially placed outside the sentence: *No have money*. In the next stage, language learners would place the subject and the negator inside the sentence but before the verb: *I do have money*.

> ### What the Research Is Telling Us ...
>
> - Fact 1: Corrective feedback is more effective when targeting a single linguistic feature at a time.
> - Fact 2: There need to be enough exposure to corrective feedback to be beneficial.
> - Fact 3: Not all forms or structures respond equally to corrective feedback.
> - Fact 4: Corrective feedback with uptake is more effective.
> - Fact 5: Corrective feedback effectiveness might depend on instructional contexts.
> - Fact 6: Elicitation is more effective if learners have some knowledge of the form/structure.
> - Fact 7: Corrective feedback is effective if it matches learners' developmental stages.

For corrective feedback to be effective, language teaching must match the feedback with L2 learners' developmental stages.

The effects of corrective feedback may not be immediate but gradual and not all grammar forms respond equally to corrective feedback. For example, language learners may notice lexical errors more effectively than errors related to our morphology system. Corrective feedback with uptake is more effective than feedback with no uptake.

Despite some mixed results in the empirical research investigating the role of corrective feedback, overall classroom research has indicated that it is desirable and helpful to provide corrective feedback without interrupting the flow of communication. Corrective feedback achieves three main things: (1) it signals an error, (2) it provides a correct model and (3) it enhances the salience of the form/structure. The question is not whether or not we should provide opportunities for interactional corrective feedback, but it is how we accomplish this in the most effective way to facilitate language development.

> **In a Nutshell ...**
> - Corrective feedback might play a facilitative role.
> - Corrective feedback (although one size does not fit all) should elicit student-generated repairs.
> - Self-correction should be encouraged.
> - Corrective feedback should be provided with some form of uptake.

---

**Task:** Does corrective feedback have a positive effect on L2 learning? If yes please explain how in your opinion.

Do you know what recast is? Can you provide an example?

What are the most effective characteristics of effective feedback? List them.

1
2
3

---

# Knowing More about the Subject

Benati, A. (2020). Key *questions in second language teaching: An introduction*. Cambridge University Press.

Benati, A. (2021). *Focus on form*. Cambridge University Press.

Benati, A., & Lee, J. (2008). *Grammar acquisition and processing instruction*. Multilingual Matters.

Benati, A., & Schwieter, J. (2019). *The Cambridge handbook of language learning*. Cambridge University Press.

Doughty C., & Williams, J. (1998). *Focus on form in classroom second language acquisition*. Cambridge University Press.

Lyster, R., & Ranta, L. (1997). Corrective feedback and learner uptake: Negotiation of form in communicative classrooms. *Studies in Second Language Acquisition, 19*, 37–66.

Nassaji, H. (2015). *The interactional feedback dimension in instructed second language learning*. Bloomsbury.

Nassaji, H., & Fotos, S. (2011). *Teaching grammar in second language classrooms*. Routledge.

Sheen, Y. (2011). *Corrective feedback, individual differences, and second language learning*. Springer.

VanPatten, B. (2020). Input processing in adult second language acquisition. In B. VanPatten, G. D. Keating & S. Wulff (eds), *Theories in second language acquisition* (pp. 105–27). Routledge.

Wong, W. (2005). *Input enhancement: From theory and research to the classroom*. McGraw-Hill.

# Further Clarifications ...

In this section, we aim to further clarify some of the terms or concepts presented in the chapter.

**The communicative approach** represents a philosophy of teaching that is based on communicative language use. The language classroom becomes an area of cooperative negotiation, joint interpretation and the sharing of expression. The language teacher is in the position to give learners the opportunity for spontaneous, unpredictable exploratory production of language when involved in classroom language tasks. The main tenets of this teaching philosophy are: (1) the meaning is emphasized over form; (2) the amount of corrective feedback is kept to a minimum letting learners express themselves; (3) comprehensible and meaningful input is provided in the classroom with the use of linguistics and non-linguistics means; (4) a variety of discourse-types activities are used with real-life materials; (5) genuine questions are used as supposed to display questions; (6) comprehension is emphasized over production with little pressure on learners to produce the target language.

**Redundant/redundancy** refers to a feature that is represented by several components of a sentence. In English, third-person -*s* is a redundant feature as far as person number is concerned. Because English almost invariably includes either a subject or a subject pronoun, third-person -*s* on the verb are redundant: it marks the same information.

**Working memory** refers to the processing space in the mind of the learner where we hold and comprehend information. The idea is that working memory has limited capacity as one can only process and store in working memory a limited amount of information before it must be dumped so that the person can continue processing new incoming information.

# 9

# How Do We Develop Effective Language Tasks for the Language Classroom?

Overview  167
What Is a Language Task?  168
How Do You Develop an Effective Listening Task?  171
How Do You Develop an Interactive Reading Task?  179
Knowing More about the Subject  194

## Overview

In this chapter an examination of what a language task is will be presented. Tasks can be effectively used to develop all language skills such as speaking, writing, listening and reading. This chapter will focus on listening and reading given that writing and speaking have been already discussed in previous chapters.

Communicative interactive tasks might facilitate language learning and provide a purpose for language use. A task can be used to achieve a specific lesson objective. Tasks (and not exercises or activities) should form the backbone of the curriculum. A psycholinguistic and effective approach to the development of listening tasks will be examined in an attempt to understand the real nature of listening in another language and develop tasks in which L2 learners are actively involved in listening to a passage for a specific purpose. A more interactive approach to reading

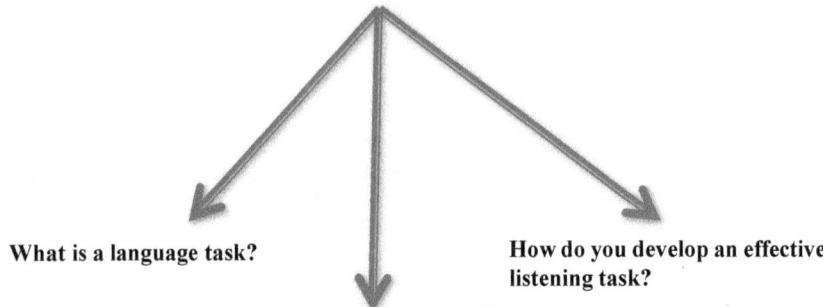

**Figure 9.1** Key questions of Chapter 9.

comprehension will also be examined. This approach is centred on the idea that L2 learners need to read to extract specific information and not to translate texts.

It is vital to train learners in developing the ability to understand written passages without understanding every single word. In the approach to reading comprehension presented in this chapter, developing reading skills is seen as developing the ability to read in another language. Language learners read texts in another language for a specific purpose. They read to gain specific information. The purpose(s) for reading must guide the language instructor's selection of texts. In addition to that, authentic material should be used. Three questions are addressed in this chapter (Figure 9.1).

Chapter 9

How do we develop effective language tasks for the classroom?

# What Is a Language Task?

Pedagogical tasks are widely used and accepted as effective language practice in contemporary language teaching. Language tasks are both meaningful and have a communicative purpose. The exact definition of a language task varies somewhat among scholars, but the two key elements are:

- Tasks involve the expression and interpretation of the meaning
- Tasks have a purpose that is not language practice

A task is a classroom activity that has a specific purpose attainable only by (1) the interaction among participants, (2) a mechanism for structuring and sequencing interaction and (3) a focus on meaning. Tasks provide learners with a purpose for language use and make language teaching more communicative. Language tasks are activities that involve understanding and processing the target language. They have specific features:

> **In a Nutshell ...**
>
> A task is a language-learning endeavour that requires language learners to:
>
> - comprehend language,
> - manipulate and
> - produce the target language following several steps.

- Provide a piece of extended discourse
- Have an information gap element
- Have an uncertainty element
- They are goal orientated
- They are real-time processing
- Require two or more autonomous participants
- Privilege the learners' use of the language

To create a communicative and effective activities the following criteria should be adopted:

- Clarify the purpose of the task
- Break down the task into sub-tasks called steps
- The teacher is the planner who is planning the task and the learners are the executors

If a language task follows the above criteria and is structured in an appropriate way, it can successfully promote communication among language learners. L2 research and theory recognize the importance of comprehensible input but view interactional modifications as important in making input comprehensible. Classroom research has proved that interactional modifications and negotiation take place more successfully in paired group activities than in teacher-fronted activities. As previously mentioned, negotiation of meaning is a form of interaction during which speakers come to terms, reach agreements, make some arrangements, solve a problem or settle an issue by conferring or discussing.

In interaction tasks, the main purpose of language use is to accomplish some language tasks and not to practise any particular form. Input will provide learners with the linguistic data necessary to develop the internal language system and output practice will ultimately help learners develop the use of the language for communicative purposes. Tasks promote communication, but the question is whether they also have a beneficial role in L2 learning. It can be argued that language tasks can facilitate language learning processes in several ways.

Firstly, in interactive tasks, learners receive and are exposed to meaningful input from a variety of sources: teachers, other learners and the task itself. More importantly, the input, both aural and written, is made comprehensible and meaningful. The input language learners are exposed to is simplified and more processable (e.g. short utterances, forms are made salient and the language is simplified). These modifications help language learners to process the target language, and it increases the chances for the successful development of their internal language system.

Secondly, in interactive tasks, learners are not engaged in mechanical output practice (e.g. drills, repetition exercises) where the language they produce is not meaningful. Interactive tasks would instead allow language learners to engage in meaningful production of language which might help them in filling the gaps in their knowledge (forms, words and structures to convey meaning) and facilitating language learning.

Thirdly, in interactive tasks, the focus is not just the expression and interpretation of meaning but also the negotiation of meaning. Providing language learners with opportunities to negotiate meaning (e.g. confirmation checks, comprehension checks) would increase the amount of language input that is comprehended and subsequently it would facilitate learning.

### What the Research Is Telling Us ...

Language interactive tasks facilitate language learning by

- Fact 1. providing language learners with comprehensible and meaningful input
- Fact 2. providing language learners with the opportunity to interact and learn language inductively
- Fact 3. providing language learners with opportunity for negotiation of meaning
- Fact 4: engaging language learners in meaningful and authentic language that promotes learning by doing
- Fact 5: engaging language learners in co-operative and collaborative learning
- Fact 6: exposing language learners to focus on form and implicit corrective feedback (e.g. recast)

The following key features of an effective task have been identified:

- A task is not a text.
- A task is a work plan. This work plan takes the form of teaching materials or ad hoc plans for activities that arise in the course of teaching.
- A task involves a primary focus on meaning.
- A task involves real-world processes of language use.
- A task can involve any of the four language skills.
- A task engages cognitive processes. The work plan requires learners to employ cognitive processes such as selecting, classifying, ordering, reasoning and evaluating information to carry out the task.
- A task has clearly defined outcomes.

# How Do You Develop an Effective Listening Task?

Language learners receive a great amount of information through listening from teachers and other interlocutors in the language classroom. Language listeners are actively involved in interpreting what they hear and bring their knowledge to the task of listening. Listening to the target language is a complex process as the listener needs to deal with several tasks at once: the language content and the speed of the language to which they are exposed.

How do listeners cope with processing content while listening? Language teachers need to consider which strategies learners use to understand language and provide listening practice in authentic situations similar to the ones encountered outside the classroom context.

Language learning depends a great deal on listening as it provides the aural input that serves as the basis for language development and enables language learners to interact. Language learners make use of two main listening strategies that help them to understand language input. The listener

> **In a Nutshell …**
>
> - Listeners are actively involved in processing language.
> - Listening consists of bottom-up and top-down processes.
> - Listening is an interactive and interpretative process.

relies on the language in the message, that is, the combination of sounds, words and grammar that creates meaning.

The first type of strategy used by listeners is bottom-up strategies that include listening for specific information and details. The second type of strategy used by learners to process information as they are listening to a passage is a top-down strategy. Top-down strategies are listener-based where the listener uses several tools including his background knowledge of the topic to interpret the message. Top-down strategies include listening to grasp the main ideas and concepts in a listening passage. When learners are able to use both top-down and bottom-up strategies they successfully interpret the meaning of the passage.

Listening is an active and productive language skill. Language learners should always engage in a listening comprehension activity to construct meanings from the message they hear. To achieve this outcome, language learners must be exposed to listening comprehension tasks in which they are actively engaged in processing language to extract meaning. Language learners must be given all the opportunities to extract the main message from the passage using clues and processing key meaningful words.

> **In a Nutshell ...**
>
> Listening consists of three main mental processes:
>
> - Perceiving
> - Attending
> - Assigning meaning

Language knowledge and topic familiarity are two key factors in helping language learners fully comprehend what they hear in the target language. Humans have three processes that are involved in understanding language: (1) perceiving the sound of the language, (2) attending to the information, (3) assigning meaning to the incoming information.

Perceiving refers to the physiological and psycholinguistic aspects of listening which include the sound entering our ears and the mind making use of processing strategies to select incoming information (see our discussion on input processing in Chapter 6). Listeners do not pay attention to everything they hear but they select the language based on internal processing strategies they use as default. What is actually processed is only a small portion of the language, at least this is the case at the beginning of the process.

Attending to the information in the input requires active concentration by the listener and exposure to language that is easy to process and it is comprehensible and meaningful.

Assigning meaning very often involves personal and linguistic matters interacting in complex ways. Research from cognitive psychology has shown that the ability to develop listening competence can't be associated only with the ability to extract meaning from incoming speech. Developing listening skills is instead a process of matching speech with what listeners already know about the topic. Language teachers must consider these findings and on one hand develop tasks to facilitate learners' activation of prior knowledge, and on the other hand, allow learners to make the appropriate inferences essential to comprehending the message.

> **In a Nutshell …**
>
> Traditional listening comprehension has several shortcomings:
> - Learners are passive listeners
> - Learners focus on linguistic elements rather than meaningful elements

Language teachers need to help learners in the following ways: (1) organizing their thoughts before their listening task begins, (2) activating language learners' background knowledge so that they can process more information and understand the message, (3) preparing language learners for listening and understand the main message to reduce the burden of comprehension for the listener. They do not need to understand every word in the passage, (4) considering the possibility to decrease or increase, depending on learners' proficiency level, the speed and level of the listening passage, (5) deciding on the complexity of the listening task, (6) considering the use of non-linguistics items in support of the listening task (e.g. pictures, visual aids).

Two types of listening interactive tasks can be designed about their purpose: (1) an interactional task and (2) a transactional task.

1. Interactional listening tasks are two-way listening tasks and (e.g. talks, and conversations) are highly contextualized involving an interactive component with a speaker.
2. Transactional listening tasks are one-way listening tasks (e.g. news, broadcasts) that are more message-oriented and are used primarily to communicate information. They require the listeners to comprehend

the message very accurately. Knowing the communicative purpose of a text will help the listener determine what to listen for and, therefore, which particular listening strategy to adopt.

In the case of the type of classroom tasks that might facilitate the development of listening comprehension skills, classroom research suggests that listening tasks should be well structured to allow active participation and interaction from the listener.

> **In a Nutshell ...**
>
> The use of interactive and meaningful listening comprehension tasks have the following effects:
>
> - Expose language learners to meaningful input
> - Expose language learners to comprehensible input
> - Expose language learners to interactive language
> - Help learners to tap into and develop listening strategies

In a traditional approach to listening, the role assigned to the language learners is simply to listen to a passage to answer a question or fill in a gap. The listener usually must process the linguistic element rather than processing the actual message contained in the passage.

In interactive tasks, the main goal of the listening task is to comprehend the meaning of the passage. Language teachers make all the possible efforts to ensure language learners understand and process language input by tapping on both bottom-up and top-down listening strategies.

The real challenge here is to develop listening tasks that will stimulate the development of listening competence while equipping learners with listening strategies. L2 learners must be engaged in listening tasks where they make simultaneous use of bottom-up and top-down strategies.

> **What the Research Is Telling Us ...**
>
> Based on L2 learning research, this is a list of tendencies that successful language listeners might display when processing language:
>
> - They tend to predict and/or guess about what they might hear or what might happen;

- They tend to focus on keywords and select the key information;
- They tend to understand the meaning of what they hear;
- They tend to reflect on what they heard and attempt to formulate an opinion, and/or to interact with a speaker, or to personalize the content of what they heard.

When we develop a listening task we should consider the following guidelines for designing effective listening tasks:

1. Language teachers should develop a listening task for a specific communicative purpose using topics that relate to language learners' familiarity, needs and interests. In these types of listening tasks, language learners would be required to extract something meaningful from a listening text;
2. Language teachers must design a listening task that will activate learners' background knowledge about a specific topic. Listeners will be able to predict or anticipate the content of the listening task (pre-listening stage). Language instructors should make use of pre-listening activities to prepare students for what they are going to hear or view. These activities assess learners' background knowledge and provide them with the background knowledge necessary for their comprehension (e.g. reviewing relevant vocabulary or grammatical structures before listening to a passage, reading something relevant to the listening task, predicting the content of the listening text, think-pair-share, brainstorming). Pre-listening activities will allow language learners to establish the main listening purpose of the passage so that they can be ready to extract the specific information they need to understand the content;
3. In listening for a specific purpose, language learners are asked to process the parts of the text that are relevant to identify the overall meaning (while-listening stage) of the listening task. This selective and contextualized approach would help learners to focus on specific parts of the text and therefore reduce the amount of information they have to process and comprehend;
4. Language teachers should define the task's instructional goal and the type of response they expect from the learner. Language learners must know what they are listening for and why. Each listening activity in a task should have clear goals such as recognizing specific aspects of the message, recognizing sounds and words, and comprehending

main ideas (while-listening stage). The pre-listening stage would help learners to make decisions about what to listen for and, subsequently, to focus attention on meaning while listening;

5. Language teachers should expose learners to a variety of activities to develop the two main listening strategies (top-down and bottom-up). While-listening activities such as looking for keywords, looking for nonverbal cues to meaning, associating the information with one existing background knowledge, guessing meaning and listening for the general gist would help learners to comprehend and process meaning.

> **In a Nutshell ...**
>
> Listening comprehension tasks consist of three stages:
> - Pre-listening stage
> - While-listening stage
> - Post-listening stage

In developing effective listening comprehension tasks, language teachers must not give learners irrelevant detailed comprehension questions and engage in tasks where learners listen and repeat everything. Instead, a listening comprehension task should be designed for a purpose and must have a clear set of procedures and a tangible outcome.

Based on these assumptions, a three-stage interactive task approach to listening comprehension is proposed.

In the pre-listening stage, language instructors should set the context, and activate learners' prior knowledge through cooperative learning tasks (e.g. brainstorming, think-pair-share). Effective pre-listening activities involve learners to predict ideas. The pre-listening stage enables learners to tap into what they already know (background knowledge) and predict key information to comprehend the text.

In the while-listening stage, language learners are required to listen for main ideas to establish the context of what they are listening to. Language learners are exposed to listening bottom-up activities (e.g. word sentence recognition, listening for the different words and forms), top-down activities (e.g. identifying the topic, understanding the meaning of a sentence) and interactive tasks (e.g. listening to a list and categorizing the words, following directions). During the while-listening stage, language instructors can develop activities in which learners are asked to match short phrases with a list of dates and/or identify the specific sentence in the listening passage.

In the post-listening stage, learners are asked to articulate their ideas and clarify meanings. Language learners are allowed to 'personalize' their understanding of the passage and monitor their progress (see listening comprehension task below).

# Listening Text

1. On 15 January 1929, Martin Luther King Jr. is born in Atlanta, Georgia, the son of a Baptist minister. King received a doctorate in theology and in 1955 helped organize the first major protest of the African American civil rights movement: the successful Montgomery Bus Boycott. Influenced by Mohandas Gandhi, he advocated civil disobedience and non-violent resistance to segregation in the South. The peaceful protests he led throughout the American South were often met with violence, but King and his followers persisted, and the movement gained momentum.
2. A powerful orator, King appealed to Christian and American ideals and won growing support from the federal government and Northern whites. In 1963, Bayard Rustin and A. Philip Randolph led the massive March on Washington for Jobs and Freedom; the event's grand finale was King's famous 'I Have a Dream' speech. Two hundred and fifty thousand people gathered outside the Lincoln Memorial to hear the stirring speech.
3. In 1964, the civil rights movement achieved two of its greatest successes: the ratification of the 24th Amendment, which abolished the poll tax, and the Civil Rights Act of 1964, which prohibited racial discrimination in employment and education and outlawed racial segregation in public facilities. Later that year, King became the youngest person to win the Nobel Peace Prize (in 2014 Malala Yousafzai became the youngest to receive the prize at age seventeen). In the late 1960s, King openly criticized US involvement in Vietnam and turned his efforts to winning economic rights for poor Americans. He was assassinated in Memphis, Tennessee, on 4 April 1968.

# Pre-Listening Task Stage

1. Everyone knows about the extraordinary life of Dr Martin Luther King. What do you know about him? Work with a partner. List what you know about him.
2. Here are some words from the passage you will hear. Listen to the teacher say them. Are you familiar with these expressions?
    - civil rights movement…
    - Baptist minister…
    - protest…
    - gained momentum…
    - nonviolent resistance…
    - racial segregation.

# While-Listening Task Stage

1. Listen to this brief bio about Martin Luther King. First, listen for dates and key events in his life. As you listen, look at the timeline below. Listen for one event for each date on the timeline. Write a short phrase for each event.
    1929 _____
    1955 _____
    1963 _____
    1964 _____
    1968 _____
2. Read these sentences. Some of these are in the passage. Listen again. Which of these phrases are in the passage? Check them.
    - He helped organize the first major protest of the African American civil rights movement.
    - While he was still in high school, he joined the civil rights movement.
    - He decided to travel to Europe to gain support.
    - He became the youngest person to win the Nobel Peace Prize
    - He was able to change racial law in the United States.
    - He was assassinated in Memphis, Tennessee.

# Post-Listening Task Stage

1. Work with a partner. Compare your timelines. Give extra information about each event.
2. Do you have any questions about the passage? Are there any new vocabulary words? Ask your teacher now. Use these phrases:
   - What does '….' mean?
   - I heard a phrase that sounded like '…..' I'm not familiar with that.
   - I couldn't catch the part after '…'
3. Listen to the passage one last time. In your own words, what is the theme of the passage? What feeling do you get when you listen to the passage?
4. What did you learn from the passage about Dr Martin Luther King's life?

---

**Task:** Develop an effective listening comprehension task keeping in mind the following phases:

- Pre-listening
- While-listening
- Post-listening

---

# How Do You Develop an Interactive Reading Task?

Reading in another language is considered an interactive process between the reader and the text. Readers must develop the competence to process and comprehend elements such as words and forms in the text and connect all the various parts of the text to understand the meaning conveyed. Words and forms in the text encode particular meanings.

Like in the case of developing listening skills, readers use both top-down and bottom-up strategies to interact with the text. Reading and comprehending can be then defined as the ability of readers to use and apply appropriate strategies to successfully comprehend a written text. Research on word recognition has indicated that recognizing a word is a necessary component of comprehending a text. However, this is not sufficient. Readers must construct meaning from the words he/she can recognize. In other words, form-meaning connections need to be made to successfully process and comprehend language. Language teachers must therefore provide opportunities for learners to make these associations.

Developing language learner's ability to comprehend written texts involves three main processes: (1) facilitating the process of recognizing words in the written text, (2) constructing meaning from a text and (3) making use of learners' background knowledge.

> ### What the Research Is Telling Us ...
> Research is telling us that in order to develop competence in reading, language learners must:
> Fact 1: Recognize words in the written input
> Fact 2: Assign meaning and make word-meaning connections
> Fact 3: Make use of language learners' background knowledge

> ### In a Nutshell ...
> Language learners make use of both bottom-up and top-down strategies to develop their reading competence in another language.

In reading comprehension, both bottom-up and top-down strategies are used. Bottom-up strategies are used by language learners to process information in the text (e.g. individual words and forms such as verbs, adjectives and the like) and interpret the meaning of this information. Top-down strategies involve processing language beyond the analysis of linguistics information (e.g. knowledge of the text structure, prior knowledge of the topic and cultural awareness about the topic in the text).

Theory and research in L2 reading have provided several important insights into how language learners understand and process information in a written text and what might facilitate their ability to read in another language (see what the research is telling us in the table below).

# What the Research Is Telling Us ...

Research in how language learners develop reading abilities has provided the following insights:

- Language learners benefit from pre-reading activities as these activities are very effective to activate their background knowledge;
- Language learners should be exposed to reading comprehension activities where they gradually bridge the gap between their knowledge and the text;
- Language learners should be helped to make connections between a form/word and its meaning in the context of reading a text;
- Learners should be exposed to reading interactive tasks using a stage-based approach where they develop their ability to comprehend the text in stages.

Several teaching and learning strategies facilitate language learners in bridging the gap between their knowledge of the topic and the written text in a language classroom activity. (1) Exploiting readers' background knowledge through brainstorming activities before reading the text might help language learners make predictions about the content and structure of the text they are going to read. (2) Skimming and scanning a text before actually reading the entire written text might help language learners to get the main ideas in the text and confirm or question previous predictions. (3) Guessing from context might help learners to process words and forms and make appropriate form-meaning connections of these unknown words/forms rather than translating word by word like in the case of traditional reading comprehension activities. (4) Paraphrasing might help language learners to summarize the main ideas and concepts in a text using their own words.

Language teachers can facilitate the use of these reading strategies in several ways. Language learners would find it difficult to process complex language and unfamiliar topics. Language teachers must select a text according to the learner's topic familiarity. They can take learners through the processes of previewing, predicting, skimming and scanning, and paraphrasing during a reading comprehension activity. They should allow enough time in the classroom for group previewing and predicting activities in preparation for a reading comprehension task (pre-reading stage). Language teachers should

> **In a Nutshell ...**
>
> There are several key steps to be considered to facilitate the language learner in reading and understanding a written text:
>
> - Language readers should have the opportunity to predict the content of the written text.
> - Language readers should gradually process and understand portions of the text as supposed to reading the all text at once.
> - Language readers should have the opportunity to connect words and the meaning of these words in the written text.

> **In a Nutshell ...**
>
> Traditional reading comprehension activities consist of the following:
>
> - Translation of a written text
> - Reading a written text followed by Q/A

develop reading interactive tasks that encourage learners to guess meaning from context and make appropriate word-meaning mappings.

Traditional reading comprehension activities which often appear in textbooks consist mainly of two types: (1) translation activities where the reader is asked to translate a written text in the target language and (ii) Q/A activities where the reader is asked to read a text (word by word) and answer a series of questions from a text. Reading comprehension should not be viewed as a translating exercise or answering a question from a written text. Instead, it should be viewed as reading in another language.

The fact that learners might not have the verbal virtuosity of a native reader means that language teachers need to utilize several strategies to help them. The reading comprehension framework presented in this chapter takes into consideration the need to guide learners in their comprehension of a text in the language classroom. In adopting a principled evidence-based approach to the teaching of reading, a series of measures need to be taken.

Language teachers should develop reading activities following a four-stage approach: (1) pre-reading stage, (2) text-interaction stage, (3) post-reading stage and (4) personalization stage. When designing a reading task, language teachers must keep in mind that they should not expect learners to process all the information in a text.

The purpose of a reading comprehension task is to bridge the gap between the reader and the information contained in the text. The tasks follow a four-stage approach with a pre-reading stage, a text-interaction stage, a post-reading stage and a personalization stage.

> **In a Nutshell ...**
>
> Interactive and meaningful reading comprehension activities consist of the following stages:
>
> - pre-reading stage
> - text-interaction stage
> - post-reading stage
> - personalization stage

1. Pre-reading activities are designed to ensure that language learners have the opportunity to activate their background knowledge relevant to the topic in the reading comprehension text:
   - brainstorming the main topics covered in the text. This can take place before reading the text and should help to predict and tease out the main content of the reading text;
   - providing subtitles and headings. This is a technique that can be used to activate learners' background knowledge and or to predict content;
   - scanning for specific information can be used in the case of a text that does not need extensive preparation. Teachers ask learners to scan the text for specific information, to skim to find the theme or main idea and to elicit information activating appropriate prior knowledge.

In the pre-reading stage, language teachers provide learners with different stimuli to predict the content of reading comprehension text. Learners are asked to read the title of the text and jot down (in pairs or group work) some possible ideas/topics they expect to find in the text. This kind of activity is designed to familiarize readers with the written text and bridge the gap between the reader and the text. Pre-reading activities serve the purpose of mainly preparing learners for reading and completing the task.

2. During the text interaction stage, language learners engage in several activities aimed at scanning for specific information in the text. Initially, readers should process the text to understand the general meaning. Learners are asked to quickly scan the text to establish whether or not they have guessed the content during pre-reading activities. In the text-interaction stage, learners explore fully the main content of a text.

Language instructors should provide a guide to this process to avoid learners reading word for word. Language instructors must make sure that learners understand what the purpose of reading is. Language learners must get the main ideas, obtain specific information and gradually understand most of the message. Recognizing the purpose of reading will help students select appropriate reading strategies. This stage consists of a combination of two types of activities: (1) management strategies in which we suggest ways to divide a text and divide it into small parts and (2) comprehension checks implemented during the guided interaction phase so that readers are monitored in an ongoing way.
3. In the post-reading stage learners are given a series of activities in which they need to organize the information in the text. Post-reading activities are designed to check and verify comprehension. The purpose of these activities is to encourage readers to learn from what they have read.
4. The personalization stage is when language teachers engage language learners in exploiting the content of the text in order to reuse the information to complete a task such as writing a letter or designing a poster. This stage is the one for language learners to apply the main concepts comprehended in the text to another context.

An interactive model for the comprehension of written language should be adopted. This model envisages that learners make a positive contribution to their language development. Based on the principles highlighted in this chapter, language teachers should be supplied with the following guidelines for the development of effective reading comprehension tasks:

- Effective reading comprehension tasks should be constructed around a purpose that has a clear significance for language learners who need to provide appropriate responses;
- Effective reading comprehension tasks should have pre-reading activities to prepare language learners for reading and activate their background knowledge;
- Effective reading comprehension tasks should use interaction activities to gradually help language learners to process the meaning of the text;
- Effective reading comprehension tasks should use post-reading activities to ensure language learners have processed and comprehended the main content of the text;

- Effective reading comprehension tasks should develop personalization activities to ensure language learners can reuse the content they have learned in the reading text in order to complete a language task of a related matter.

---

**Task:** What is the difference between reading for translating and reading in another language?

Effective reading comprehension tasks include the following phases:

- Pre-reading
- In-text interaction
- Post-reading
- Personalization

Using these four phrases, develop an interactive reading comprehension task.

Please see two examples of interactive reading comprehension tasks below.

---

**Pre-Reading Stage**

    a. Discuss with your partners the following issues around 'euthanasia'

- What do you think of 'euthanasia'?
- What are the risks of making it legal?
- What would you do to tackle this issue?

    b. Read the tile of the text and write a couple of ideas/concepts you are predicting to find in the main text.

Why we should make euthanasia legal

- 
- 

Text Interaction Stage

    c. Read the text quickly to find out whether you have rightly guessed the ideas.

Why we should make euthanasia legal

1. The issue of euthanasia, or assisted dying, is incredibly controversial and there are legitimate concerns on either side of the debate. The starting point has to be in the law, which at present is failing, as shown by the recurrence of cases in the courts that often place relatives, already dealing with the painful loss of a loved one, in the middle of distressing legal battles. There is a desire – whether we like it or not – among several patients at the end of often terrible battles with debilitating, incurable diseases to end their suffering with the support of their relatives. To deny this right is to prolong the suffering of individuals and families, something that I can simply not condone.
2. I do accept though that this is not like any other clinical decision – and that if society is to offer this solemn choice it must also build in safeguards to its laws that not only rectify the inadequacies of the current situation but also protect the vulnerable, the weak and all those – doctors and nurses included – who are involved in this incredibly difficult situation. As a start, we must enact legislation to decriminalize acts of euthanasia and physician-assisted suicide. Some of the reasons that are compelling enough for us to change our laws are:
3. Prevention of cruelty and protection of human rights
   To allow terminally ill individuals to end their life is the only humane, rational and compassionate choice. The current prohibitions require a person with great physical and/or mental suffering to continue to endure their suffering against their wishes, which cannot be right. The right to life and the right to private and family life under the European convention on human rights should be interpreted broadly to include decisions about the quality of life, including decisions about death if life is no longer one of quality.
4. Regulatory Control
   The terminally ill are travelling abroad to countries where the right to end life in terminal cases is recognized and is lawful. We cannot regulate the laws of foreign lands. We must make provisions within our laws to regulate this issue within our boundaries under our control and supervision. We must not prosecute loved ones for 'encouraging or assisting' suicide who enable or assist a terminally ill individual to travel abroad to end his or her life lawfully.

5. Ambiguity in the application of the current law
The current law conflicts with the law as it is being enforced. If the laws as written were being enforced, over a hundred people would have been prosecuted for accompanying their loved ones abroad to help them end their lives. This ambiguity and uncertainty leave all concerned, including physicians, unprotected.
6. Discriminatory effect of the laws
The ability of the wealthy to travel to countries where it is lawful for the terminally ill to end their lives has the discriminatory impact of treating the haves and have-nots unequally.
7. The safeguards
Many people are opposed to legislation that would allow 'end-of-life' choices. But our concerns relating to abuses and protection of the vulnerable can be addressed by ensuring that certain objective safeguard conditions are met before allowing a terminally ill individual from exercising his or her right to die with dignity. Some of the safeguards include the following:

The patient must be terminally ill.
The patient must be an adult.
The patient must be mentally competent.
The patient must be in severe pain.
Two independent physicians must be satisfied that the above conditions are present.

8. In conclusion, the only humane choice is to allow individuals who are suffering to choose to end their suffering. Further, the discrepancies in the laws as they exist and how they are being enforced have led to uncertainty. This uncertainty leaves the doctors, their patients and patient's loved ones unprotected. If we do not address these issues openly and head-on, we will have continued uncertainty and unregulated practice of euthanasia or assisted suicide with the fear of prosecution hanging over the heads of all concerned. The goals of the medical profession should continue to remain one of saving lives but this should not be at the expense of compassion and a terminally ill individual's right to choose to end his or her life and die with dignity.

d. Read the four sections of the text and reflect on its content. For each section write a short paragraph summarizing the main meaning.

- 
- 
- 
- 
- 
- 

e. Based on what you have read indicate whether these statements are true or false.

|  | True | False |
|---|---|---|
| 1. The terminally ill should have the right to end their life | ☐ | ☐ |
| 2. The terminally ill travel to certain countries to end their life | ☐ | ☐ |
| 3. Many people support euthanasia | ☐ | ☐ |
| 4. To end life the patient can be a child | ☐ | ☐ |
| 5. The role of the doctor is to assist in life termination | ☐ | ☐ |

f. Find the synonymous of the following words in the text.

| WORDS | SYNONYMOUS IN THE TEXT |
|---|---|
| 1. nobility | |
| 2. mercy killing | |
| 3. legitimize | |
| 4. worrying | |
| 5. compassionate | |

| WORDS | SYNONYMOUS IN THE TEXT |
|---|---|
| 6. deficiencies | |
| 7. ban | |
| 8. control | |
| 9. protection | |
| 10. imposed | |

**Post-Reading Stage**

g. Step 1: Work with your partner and identify four possible solutions to the problem of 'euthanasia'.

- 
- 
- 
- 

Step 2: Working with the other groups in class, prepare a poster against or in favour of 'euthanasia'.

**Personalization Stage**

h. Working in groups, prepare the questions for an interview on the main issues concerning euthanasia.

Questions

_____

_____

_____

_____

_____

Another example of an interactive meaningful reading comprehension task is provided below in the case of French-language teaching.

**Stade de la pré-lecture**

Discutez avec vos partenaires sur les questions suivantes autour de 'racisme'

- Que pensez-vous de la question de «racisme»?
- Quelles sont les raisons?
- Que feriez-vous pour résoudre le problème?

Lire la tuile du texte et écrire quelques idées / concepts que vous prédisent à trouver dans le texte principal.

### Le racisme et la discrimination

- 
- 

**Stade de lecture**

Lire le texte rapidement. Pour savoir si vous avez deviné juste titre les idées.

### Le racisme et la discrimination

1. Le racisme possède plusieurs dimensions. On peut le définir comme l'ensemble des idées, des attitudes et des actes qui visent à inférioriser les personnes des minorités ethnoculturelles, sur les plans social, économique et politique, les empêchant ainsi de participer pleinement à la société.

Le racisme est aujourd'hui essentiellement revendiqué par les groupes néo-nazis et suprémacistes. Cette idéologie présente un groupe culturel, défini par la couleur de la peau ou par des caractéristiques culturelles ou religieuses, comme supérieur aux autres et qui doit donc être le seul à jouir pleinement des droits garantis par l'État. Cette idéologie ne recueille plus l'appui des États démocratiques modernes, à la suite des crimes et des atrocités qu'elle a suscités dans le passé.

Cependant, il persiste encore des préjugés et de la discrimination à l'égard des personnes des communautés culturelles dans les sociétés contemporaines.

2. La discrimination est une distinction, exclusion ou préférence fondée sur les motifs interdits par la *Charte québécoise des droits et libertés des droits et libertés de la personne* qui a pour effet de détruire ou compromettre l'exercice des droits et libertés. Ces motifs sont: la« race », la couleur, le sexe, la grossesse, l'orientation sexuelle, l'état civil, l'âge sauf dans la mesure prévue par la loi, la religion, les convictions politiques, la langue, l'origine ethnique ou nationale, la condition sociale, le handicap ou l'utilisation d'un moyen pour pallier ce handicap. La discrimination

peut se manifester autant par l'exclusion que par le harcèlement ou un traitement défavorable.

Le harcèlement est une forme particulière de discrimination. Il peut se manifester, à l'égard d'une personne ou d'un groupe de personnes, notamment par des paroles, des actes ou des gestes répétés, à caractère vexatoire ou méprisant. Un seul acte grave engendrant un effet nocif continu peut aussi constituer du harcèlement.

3. La discrimination directe se présente lorsque la distinction, l'exclusion ou la préférence se fonde clairement sur l'un des motifs interdits par la Charte québécoise. Ainsi, un employeur qui refuse d'embaucher un Noir du seul fait qu'il est Noir fait de la discrimination directe.

La discrimination indirecte provient de l'application d'une pratique en apparence neutre et applicable à tous, mais qui a des effets préjudiciables envers les groupes définis sur la base des motifs de discrimination interdits par la Charte. Ainsi, fixer une taille élevée pour l'accès à certains métiers, et ce, sans raison liée à la nature du travail, discrimine indirectement les femmes et les personnes des communautés culturelles, dont la taille moyenne est inférieure. Aucune intention de discriminer n'est ici en cause. La discrimination provient de normes et de pratiques arbitraires souvent héritées sans examen critique d'époques plus anciennes. L'analyse des pratiques est donc nécessaire pour la dépister.

4. Le racisme et la discrimination tendent à diminuer les chances des personnes qui en sont victimes d'avoir un travail à la hauteur de leurs compétences et les mêmes possibilités de promotion. Lorsqu'elles ne réussissent pas à surmonter les obstacles professionnels auxquels elles sont confrontées et à s'intégrer de façon durable sur le marché du travail, leur niveau de vie est affecté. Elles ontdonc un accès moindre aux services publics et privés comme le logement, l'éducation et les loisirs notamment.

Selon l'Organisation mondiale de la santé, le racisme a un impact négatif sur la santé mentale, car il crée de la détresse psychologique. En outre, les personnes qui se sentent rejetées par la société en raison des préjugés dont elles font l'objet risquent d'avoir un faible sentiment d'appartenance à cette société qui est pourtant la leur.

Le racisme et la discrimination ont aussi un impact négatif sur la société qui les tolère. Les institutions, les entreprises et la société en général, se privent du potentiel, des talents et des ressources des personnes qui sont exclues en raison des préjugés.

## Stade texte interaction
Lisez les quatre sections du texte et de réfléchir sur son contenu. Pour chaque section écrire un court paragraphe résumant la signification principale.

- 
- 
- 
- 

Basé sur ce que vous avez lu indiquer si ces déclarations sont vraies ou fausses.

|  | Vrai | Faux |
|---|---|---|
| 1. Le racisme pourrait avoir un impact sur la santé des peuples | ☐ | ☐ |
| 2. racismes directes ou indirectes sont très similaires | ☐ | ☐ |
| 3. L'ignorance est la principale raison pour les gens d'être raciste | ☐ | ☐ |
| 4. Le racisme a un impact négatif sur l'économie | ☐ | ☐ |

Trouver le synonyme des mots suivants dans le texte.

Mots                                   Synonymes dans le texte

1. Difficultés
2. Motifs
3. Buts
4. Sentiment d'appartenance

## Stade de post-lecture
Étape 1: Travailler avec votre partenaire et identifier les quatre solutions possibles au problème de 'racisme'.

Étape 2: Travailler avec les autres groupes de la classe de préparer une affiche contre le «racisme»

## Stade de personnalisation
Travailler en groupe de préparer une entrevue / questionnaire sur les principales questions concernant avec racisme.

**Figure 9.2** Interactive reading and comprehension task.

| Questions | |
|---|---|
|  |  |
|  |  |
|  |  |
|  |  |
|  |  |

---

**Quiz:** Take the following short quiz to see what you have learned in this module. Answers are provided at the end.

a. A main difference between activities and tasks is that tasks …

   1. Always have a linguistic purpose
   2. Always have a communicative purpose
   3. Always have a focus on language practice

b. Reading comprehension tasks are effective if …

   1. Readers bridge the gap between the text and their knowledge
   2. Read and translate
   3. Read and answer questions

c. Listening comprehension tasks are effective if …

   1. Listeners interact with the passage
   2. Listeners answer questions
   3. Listeners are passive listeners

---

# Takeaways from This Chapter

- Tasks are the quintessential communicative event in contemporary language teaching. They are both meaningful and have a communicative purpose.
- A task is a language-learning endeavour that requires students to (1) comprehend, (2) manipulate and (3) produce the target language as they perform some set of work plans.
- Listening comprehension tasks consist of three stages:

> Pre-listening
> While-listening
> Post-listening
>
> - Interactive and meaningful approaches to listening comprehension engage learners in:
>
>   Exposure to meaningful and comprehensive input
>   Interaction
>   Communication
>   Develop listening strategies
>
> - Reading comprehension communicative tasks are a good example of interactive tasks and should substitute traditional reading and comprehension practice.
>
>   - Developing reading comprehension competence involves the interaction of a variety of knowledge sources
>   - An interactive model for the comprehension of written language has been proposed
>   - This model envisages that language learners make a positive contribution to their learning
>
> - The interactive and meaningful framework for developing reading comprehension tasks comprises different stages:
>
>   i. pre-reading stage
>   ii. text-interaction stage
>   iii. post-reading stage
>   iv. personalization stage

# Knowing More about the Subject

Anderson, N. (1999). *Exploring second language reading: Issues and strategies.* Heinle & Heinle.

Brantmeier, C. (2009). *Crossing languages and research methods: Analyses of adult foreign language reading.* Information Age Publishing.

Brown, S. (2011). *Listening myths.* University of Michigan Press.

Dave, W., & Willis, J. (2007). *Doing task-based teaching.* Oxford University Press.

Ellis, R. (2003). *Task-based language learning and teaching*. Oxford University Press.
Grabe, W. (2009). *Reading in a second language: Moving from theory to practice*. Cambridge University Press.
Field, J. (2008). *Listening in the language classroom*. Cambridge University Press.
Lee, J. (2000). *Tasks and communicating in language classrooms*. McGraw-Hill.
Long, M. (2017). Interaction in the L2 classroom. In J. Leontas (ed.), *TESOL encyclopedia of English language teaching*. Wiley/TESOL International.
Long, M. (2015). *Second language acquisition and task-based language teaching*. Wiley-Blackwell.
Nunan, D. (2004). *Task-based language teaching*. Cambridge University Press.
Polio, C. (2018). *Teaching second language writing*. Routledge.
Richards, J. C. (2012). *Tips for teaching listening*. Pearson.
Robinson, P. (2011). Task-based language learning: A review of issues. *Language Learning, 61*, 1–36.
Rost, M. (2002). *Teaching and researching listening. Applied linguistics in Applied linguistics in action*. Longman.
Rost, M., & Wilson, J. (2013). *Active listening*. Pearson.
Samuda, V., & Bygate, M. (2008). *Tasks in second language learning*. Palgrave Macmillan.
Wilson, J. J. (2008). *How to teach listening*. Pearson Longman.
Williams, J. (2005). *Teaching writing in second and foreign language classrooms*. McGraw-Hill.
Willis, D., & Willis, J. (2007). *Doing task-based teaching*. Oxford University Press.
Zhao, H. H., & Anderson N. J. (2009). *Second language reading research and instruction: Crossing the boundaries*. University of Michigan Press.

# Further Clarifications ...

In this section, we aim to further clarify some of the terms or concepts presented in the chapter.

**Interaction** refers in this chapter to conversations between learners and others as these interactions might affect learning. Through interactions, learners may be led to notice things they wouldn't notice otherwise and this noticing can affect acquisition. How learners are led to notice things can happen in several ways, including the following: (1) the other speaker adjusts his or her speech due to perceived difficulties in learner comprehension, (2) the other speaker indicates in some way that the learner has produced something non-native-like (corrective feedback).

**Negotiation of meaning** in this chapter refers to when there is a communication breakdown that triggers some kind of clarification of a speaker's intended message. The purpose of negotiation is to resolve the breakdown.

# 10

# How Do We Best Use Technology in the Language Classroom?

---

Overview 197

What Is the Role of Technology in Language Learning? 197

What Are the Main Pedagogies? 202

    Computer-Mediated Communication 203

    Computer-Assisted Language Learning 203

Knowing More about the Subject 204

## Overview

In this chapter an examination of the role and use of technology in language learning will be examined. Technology is a tool which can, if used appropriately, enhance language learning. This chapter will also present and examine some of the key technologies which have been used and integrated into language teaching. Two key questions (Figure 10.1) have been raised.

## What Is the Role of Technology in Language Learning?

The role of technology in language learning and teaching has grown since the 1960s to become a key part of the learning process in and out of the

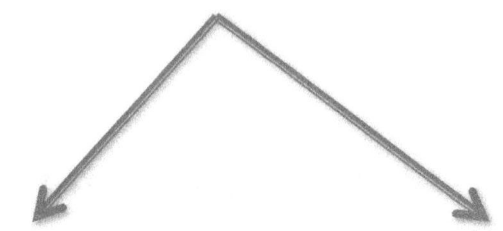

What is the role of technology in language learning?

What are the main pedagogies?

**Figure 10.1** Key questions of Chapter 10.

classroom. Almost every language teacher makes use of some form of technology in the language classroom.

The main role of technology is to provide support for language learners. Technology is a tool to help language learners develop and improve language skills, and communicate in the target language.

> **In a Nutshell ...**
>
> The role of technology in language learning is to facilitate:
>
> - exposure to language
> - interaction with the language
> - the development of language skills

The development of technology in language learning is mainly driven by the need to enhance the opportunities for successful learning by providing the kind of input, output and interactions needed to facilitate success. The questions are:

Do language learners benefit from the use of technology? How does the use of technology and technology-based pedagogies compare to classroom-based face-to-face practices? Overall, the results of research investigating and comparing technology conditions versus classroom face-to-face conditions have indicated that the use of technology is beneficial to language learners and that learners using technology perform better than the ones with no technology exposure. The integration of task-based language teaching with the use of technology has demonstrated that the use of communicative language tasks through online chat modalities is more effective than face-to-face interactions in the classroom.

Overall, the results of this comparative research have demonstrated that technology had positive effects on learners making them more engaged and motivated.

What are the main benefits? The first benefit for language learners and learning is improving motivation. There is evidence that language learners are motivated as they can work in different ways and they become more autonomous learners feeling that they can shape the learning process. There is evidence that the use of technology makes learning more motivating, enjoyable and interesting.

> **In a Nutshell ...**
>
> The main benefits of using technology are:
> - improving motivation
> - improving self-confidence
> - improving cooperation
> - improving language skills
> - providing unlimited access to input
> - reducing language anxiety

This sense of self-confidence has certainly led to the second main benefit of using technology in language learning which is the fact that individual learners become more responsible for their own learning and language teachers play more of the role of the planner and facilitator. Language learning is more learner-centred than teacher-centred. There is evidence that the use of technology makes learning more interactive and engaging.

The third benefit of technology, which derives from the previous one, is the fact that language learners become more cooperative in their learning. They become co-workers in assisting language teachers in the learning and teaching process. They can work together to integrate the technology element in the classroom setting.

The fourth benefit of using technology is its direct effects on developing language skills. There is evidence that it has positive effects on improving learners' reading, speaking and writing skills. Language learners become faster and more effective learners as the internet, for instance, is user-friendly and provides a favourable and convenient learning platform for learners.

The fifth benefit is that the online language learning environment provides a rich exposure to meaningful and authentic input. Technology helps L2 learners to access various learning materials which are useful to promote language learning. Accessibility to language input is a key advantage of online language learning.

The sixth benefit is that language anxiety is reduced. The use of technology in language learning compared to traditional face-to-face instruction creates less anxiety among language learners. In online learning, small group collaboration increases confidence in L2 learners by providing them with the opportunity to customize their learning and become more motivated and autonomous learners.

How do we best integrate technology?

Technology enables language teachers to adapt classroom activities, thus enhancing the language learning process. Technology continues to grow in importance as a tool to help teachers facilitate language learning for their learners. Language teachers are planners and architects who do make isolated use of technology but aim at successful integration of technology in their teaching approach.

> **In a Nutshell ...**
>
> The best ways to integrate technology with language instruction are:
>
> - careful planning
> - careful alignment to curriculum and a language teaching approach

The main guidelines for language teachers to best integrate technology in their teaching are the following:

- Language teachers should play the role of planner and architect in integrating technology into their teaching to ensure comprehensible and meaningful input and opportunities for meaningful output are provided.
- Language teachers should integrate technology into their teaching to develop learners' language skills.
- Language teachers must align the use of technology to curriculum and language teaching approaches such as task-based and communicative language teaching.

Some of the principles for effective language teaching highlighted in this textbook are:

1. to provide rich, comprehensible and meaningful input;
2. to provide a focus on form to facilitate form-meaning connections;
3. to provide effective corrective feedback;

4. to promote cooperative and collaborative learning through interactions and negotiation of meaning;
  5. to promote the use of interactive and communicative language tasks as the backbone of the curriculum.

How do we integrate technology into this ideal and effective framework of language teaching?

  1. Technology can facilitate the exposure to good quality and quantity input for acquisition. The internet provides infinite and natural access to a target language input. L2 learners can access meaningful language input through aural, social and visual media. L2 learners can also be exposed to rich and meaningful input through games. If the activities are designed to exclusively use the target language, a natural need is created for learners to understand what they hear and interact with each other using the target language. The use of computer-assisted language learning (CALL) provides the advantage to expose L2 learners to richer, meaningful input through authentic language materials. The software and the internet can expose L2 learners to a high quantity of native-like languages. Language learning materials in the form of visual, audio and textual forms are brought together and made available on the website so that L2 learners have access to these resources (e.g. search engines, multimedia resources, podcasts) online.
  2. Technology can help L2 learners to intake better input in terms of making appropriate form-meaning connections. Language teachers can have access to online programmes to provide a focus on form practice. The use of digital materials has the advantage to provide L2 learners with visual and verbal exposure at the same time. Digital material can enhance linguistic features in the input and provide the opportunity to repeat exposure to the language input in focus.
  3. Technology (e.g. computer activities) can provide L2 learners with instant corrective feedback. Language teachers can have access to online programmes which can provide very tailored and implicit feedback which can lead to self-correction and understanding of the principle behind the correct use of language. Computer-mediated communication (CMC) encourages interaction opportunities in which learners' reflection and utterance are fostered.

4. The use of technology can facilitate language interactions. CMC technologies can provide L2 learners with communication opportunities beyond the constraints of the classroom (e.g. multimedia interaction with open communities and social networking).
5. The use of technology tools provides the opportunity to create an optimal task-based language learning environment, which is interactive, motivating, highly contextualized, task-oriented and authentic. Therefore, online task-based language learning with rich multimedia experience is increasingly being used.

> **What the Research Is Telling Us ... and Takeaways from This Chapter**
>
> The use of technology has positive effects on L2 learners' attitudes, self-confidence and motivation.
>
> The use of technology promotes autonomous and independent language learning.
>
> The use of technology provides L2 learners with opportunities for exposure to meaningful and rich native-language input.
>
> The use of technology can facilitate effective exposure to focus on form and corrective feedback.
>
> The use of technology tools provides the opportunity to create an optimal task-based language learning environment.

# What Are the Main Pedagogies?

> **In a Nutshell ...**
>
> Computer-assisted language learning (CALL) is a new tool and technique that can help students improve their language skills.

The language teacher is responsible for using and integrating technology in the most effective ways to enhance the opportunity for learners to learn languages effectively. Very often a distinction is made between CMC pedagogy and CALL.

# Computer-Mediated Communication

CMC refers to any written, audio or visual interactions (e.g. Facebook, Google Talk, WhatsApp) between an individual and a computer through telecommunication technology. CMC is of two main types: synchronous and asynchronous. The synchronous mode allows for real-life conversations, immediate comments, sound exposure and incidental language learning. The asynchronous mode, in contrast, gives the learner more autonomy; learners can send or respond to a message at different times.

What are the benefits of CMC? Research in this field has indicated several benefits:

1. improving motivation among learners
2. promoting reflecting learning
3. enhancing learner autonomy
4. fostering collaborating learning
5. increasing exposure to input and interaction
6. increasing opportunities for communication

1. CMC offers language learners the opportunity to interact with real people in the target language in a less anxious environment than it is in face-to-face condition in the language classroom. There is evidence that shows that CMC increases linguistic competence and grammar development.

2. CMC provides language learners with time to reflect on their learning and prepare a response/message.

3. CMC offers language learners to engage with new technologies and become autonomous learners.

4. CMC fosters language learners' cooperation and interaction during online language tasks, for example.

5. CMC offers language teachers the opportunity of integrating their teaching with computer and online tools to provide exposure to rich input and to foster language interaction and opportunities for negotiating meaning.

6. CMC allows language learners to interact and communicate with other interlocutors. It facilitates skill development and attention to linguistic forms.

# Computer-Assisted Language Learning

CALL is a new tool and technique that can help students improve their language skills. Under CALL, there are several technological tools: (1)

designing and creating CALL software is a major tool in assisting language learning and (2) the internet has transformed the nature of CALL. The internet provides a worldwide hypertext system enabling the user to branch to different pages on a computer anywhere in the world simply by a click. The tools used by language teachers through web applications include image storage and sharing, social bookmarking, discussion lists, blogs, wikis, social networking, chat rooms, podcasting or recording, usually part of a themed series, which can be downloaded from a website to a media player or computer, audio tools, video sharing applications and screen-capture tools, animation tools –comic strips, movies – and so on; (3) a virtual world is an online community that takes the form of a computer-based simulated environment through which users can interact with one another and use and create objects; (4) human language technology is used in electronic dictionaries to enable L2 learners to find out how words are pronounced. There is enough support to suggest the effectiveness of CALL in promoting language skills. CALL is such a concept that favours both the teacher and the learner. New technological advancement shows the way ahead to more progress in terms of CALL.

# Knowing More about the Subject

Chapelle, C. A. (2017). Evaluation of technology and language learning. In C. A. Chapelle & S. Sauro (eds), *The handbook of technology and second language teaching and learning* (pp. 378–92). Wiley-Blackwell.

Chapelle, C. A., & Jamieson, J. (2008). *Tips for teaching with CALL: Practical approaches to computer-assisted language learning*. Pearson Education.

Gonzaález-Lloret, M., & Ortega, L. (2014). Towards technology-mediated TBLT: An introduction. In M. Gonzaá lez-Lloret & L. Ortega (eds), *Technology-mediated TBLT: Researching technology and tasks* (pp. 1–22). John Benjamins.

Jamieson, J., & Chapelle, C. A. (2010). Evaluating CALL use across multiple contexts. *System, 38*, 357–69.

Jamieson, J., & Musumeci, M. (2017). Integrating assessment with instruction through technology. In C. A. Chapelle & S. Sauro (eds), *The handbook of technology and second language teaching and learning* (pp. 293–316). Wiley-Blackwell.

White, C. J. (2017). Distance language teaching with technology. In C. A. Chapelle & S. Sauro (eds), *The handbook of technology and second language teaching and learning* (pp. 134–48). Wiley-Blackwell.

# 11

# Frequently Asked Questions

## What Should I Read to Improve My Classroom Teaching?

Language teachers have great expectations from research and theory in language learning. They look at the possible implications of this research for improving classroom teaching. However, one of the obstacles is being able to comprehend research and theory published in specialized journals. Research papers usually present empirical research and provide critical and theoretical commentaries. The challenge for teachers is not only to identify the appropriate reading but how to read the relevant papers. Below there is a list of the key components of a research paper that teachers should be aware of when embarking on reading.

**Title:** The title provides the nature and keywords of the study undertaken.

**Abstract**: The abstract provides a synthesis of the research presented in the study.

**Background:** The background section is used to achieve two things: (1) to state the importance of the topic investigated; (2) to highlight the gap in the specific research field and indicate the motivation of the study.

**Research questions/hypotheses:** The review of previous empirical and theoretical research provided in the background section leads to the research questions/hypotheses of the study.

**Design:** The design used for the study is presented in detail so that the reader has a very clear idea of the procedure used by the researcher to conduct the study. Common components of this section are (1) description of the population of the study; (2) information on the overall procedure adopted in the study; (3) procedures used to collect data (e.g. materials, assessments, scoring) and (4) procedures used to analyse data (e.g. statistical analysis, qualitative measures to analyse data).

**Results:** In this section, the researcher reports on the main findings of the study providing a summary of what has been found.

**Discussion/Conclusion:** In the final part of the study, the researcher provides a summary statement of the results obtained from the research and discusses the meaning of the research findings in the context of the previous literature. The researcher also provides an analysis/reflection of the main results in a broader context and perspective. The final part includes the following sections:

- Analysis of the contribution and significance of the results to the general area of research
- The theoretical, methodological, practical and pedagogical implications of the results obtained
- Recommendations made by the researcher
- Limitations of study undertaken
- Suggestions for further research

**References/Appendices:** The bibliography section contains the sources and references used and consulted in the study. Appendices include additional material used during the study such as tests, raw data, interviews, questionnaires or any other procedures used which is too detailed to be included in the main body of the empirical research paper.

Below are some guidelines on how to tackle empirical research papers which might prove to be a challenge to read.

**Reading the abstract.** What information about the study will you be able to capture?

**Reading the background section.** From this section, the following information needs to be processed and understood:

What is the main focus of the study? What theoretical issue the study is attempting to address? What are previous research findings telling us? Is there a particular 'gap' in the existing knowledge the study is trying to address?

**Reading the research questions/hypotheses.** Note the following:

- What are the main variables under investigation in the study?
- What is the researcher trying to prove?

**Reading the design section.** Note the following elements in the study:

- Who are the participants?
- What is the overall procedure of the study?
- What are the instruments used to collect data?
- What are the analysis procedures used?

**Reading the results section.** From this section, the following information needs to be processed and understood:

- What are the main findings of the study?
- How is the data analysis presented?

**Reading the discussion and conclusion section.** Note the following:

- What are the answers to the research questions?
- Are the results interpreted?
- Are they consistent or inconsistent with previous research?
- What are the limitations, implications and avenues for further research?
- Is there something that should have been done differently?

**Task:** Read a classroom-based study and complete the following table.

| | |
|---|---|
| Purpose | |
| Questions | |
| Design | |
| Results | |
| Interpretation | |
| Implications | |
| Limitations/future research | |

# How Do I Make My Classroom Teaching More Innovative and Effective?

Language teachers make several decisions when they begin to teach a language course. They decide, for example, on the textbook to use. In making such a decision, they are constrained by their knowledge, experience and by the existing curriculum standards, assessment rules and guidelines provided by institutions and professional organizations. In addition, their decisions are driven and informed by several factors such as the age and proficiency of the students, the curriculum they need to cover and the availability of teaching materials. Language teachers don't often have a full understanding of what language is and how language acquisition grows in our minds. This limitation in their knowledge means that they might develop an overall limited understanding of language development that looks like the following:

- people learn languages by studying, memorizing, practising and taking tests. One of the existing beliefs is that language is learned like any other skill such as playing tennis or driving a car;
- language teaching should facilitate the development of communicative skills through Question/Answer (Q/A) activities or through the use of open-ended questions which engage students in speaking;
- language rules and grammar presented in language textbooks must be what we acquire and what wind up in our heads. Most language textbooks provide activities following a traditional approach when it comes to the teaching of grammar. Explanations about grammar rules are normally followed by mechanical drill practice;
- vocabulary can be largely taught and acquired by repetition and memorization; errors made by learners should be immediately corrected as they cause bad habits.

These beliefs are in most cases reinforced by existing teacher education curricula as the nature of language and language learning are largely absent from teachers' formal education. In this scenario, language becomes a subject matter similar to history, maths or science. The language teacher only needs general principles of education and learning and makes decisions without taking into consideration the actual nature of language and how language is acquired over time. In this scenario, language pedagogy is not informed by the main theories and research findings on how language development happens. Therefore, language teachers tend to pursue a non-evidence-based approach to language pedagogy largely driven by their experience and limited knowledge.

What do we know about L2 learning?

L2 learning is input-dependent (comprehensible and meaningful input) and it is affected by internal and universal mechanisms of language. L2 learning involves the development of an implicit, abstract, complex, universal and constrained language system. Explicit knowledge does not turn into implicit knowledge, and skill acquisition is different from the creation of an implicit system. It is the implicit system that learners must tap into to create and produce real language.

Any consideration for language pedagogy should, minimally, account for these observations. To move forward and bring real innovation while fulfilling language teachers' expectations we need to address the following key question: How do we reconnect to L2 learning to ensure we achieve/provide innovative language teaching to our students of the future?

Several steps need to be taken to reconnect to the theory and research in L2 learning to positively influence language pedagogy.

Firstly, we need to develop appropriate teacher education programmes to drive a change in practices and policies as far as language curriculum is concerned. Curriculum or language teaching materials must be genuinely informed by what we know about language and language learning. An innovative approach to language pedagogy should address some of the main pedagogical questions raised by language teachers, and it should be guided and informed by theory and empirical evidence in L2 learning. For real language teaching innovation, we should consider a principled and evidence-based approach to language pedagogy guided and informed by theory and evidence. We need to incorporate both an introduction to language and linguistics and a L2 learning module in a teacher training programme.

Secondly, language scientists have the responsibility to continue to carry out appropriate and sound empirical research in L2 learning. This type of research would need to make use of online psycholinguistics and neurolinguistics methods such as eye-tracking, self-paced reading, and event-related potentials (ERPs) to investigate the role of and nature of language teaching and measure the development of implicit knowledge.

Thirdly, we need to recognize that there is a qualitative difference between explicit and implicit knowledge of the language. For the research to advance, it needs to consider ways in which to assess and test implicit knowledge along with a consideration of what implicit knowledge is.

Fourthly, language teachers must be encouraged to actively conduct their investigations in the language classroom to test the effectiveness of new and innovative pedagogy. As we look to the future, we need to conduct research into how language is represented in the mind/brain, how it is comprehended and produced and how universals and bilingualism affect the human mind-brain. The mission of researchers and practitioners is to change the idea and the myths that language is a list of rules, that a paradigm is a way language is represented in the mind/brain, that communication can be reduced to the Q/A paradigm, that explicitly teaching grammar and vocabulary is necessary or even beneficial and that practice is a key fact to learn language.

An effective language teaching pedagogy is one based on and informed by theory and empirical research in L2 learning. Although research in L2 acquisition mainly focuses on learners and learning, the findings from this research have clear implications for language teachers and teaching. Working towards a more principled and evidence-based approach to language pedagogy means the following:

- Having a good working definition of communication.
- Having a good understanding of the role and nature of language.
- Having a good understanding of how language learning happens.

# What Are the Main Misconceptions in Language Learning and Classroom Teaching?

Unfortunately, the field of L2 learning theory and research is full of misconceptions about the nature and role of language learning. A list is provided below.

1. Language is like any other complex mental task such as driving a car, or playing chess, and it is learned via the same domain-general mechanisms.
2. Explicit knowledge turns into implicit knowledge.
3. Instruction makes a difference.
4. Learning a second language is entirely different from L1 learning.
5. Output plays a key role in language learning.

These misconceptions about language learning have produced a series of misconceptions about language teaching. See the list below.

1. Communication can be equated to the Question/Answer paradigm.
2. Grammar rules should be taught and the explanation should be followed by mechanical output practice (drills).
3. Explicit error correction has a positive effect on language learning.
4. Vocabulary should be taught by repetition and memorization.

# What Are the Main Facts in Language Learning and Classroom Teaching?

Research and theory in L2 learning have determined key facts about L2 learning and some direct positive implications for language teaching.

## Facts in Second Language Learning

1. Language learning is special and it is not learned in the same way as another complex mental phenomenon. Humans are hardwired to learn the language and have cognitive mechanisms specifically designed to deal with language. Language learning is constrained (processing and linguistic constraints).
2. Language learning involves the development of an implicit, abstract and complex language system.
3. Skill learning is different from the creation of an implicit system. There are no mechanisms (no evidence for this) that turn explicit into implicit learning.
4. The development of the language system has the following characteristics: it is slow, it is order-like (e.g. *-ing* is learned before *-s*), it is stage-like (e.g. *No drink* emerges before *I don't drink*), it consists of different processes (only a small proportion of input becomes intake), it is constrained by learner-internal processing strategies (e.g. learners process words before grammatical forms in the input). Instruction has a limited role and language is mainly learned through exposure to comprehensible and meaningful input.

5. Instruction does not affect the route of acquisition but it might facilitate the rate (speed in the way language is learned). There are also some universal features of language (Universal Grammar) that interacts with input data.
6. L1 and L2 learning are similar in terms of language processes. The main difference is that L2 learners are not exposed to the same quality and quantity of input as L1 learners are exposed to.
7. The basic data for L2 learning is comprehensible and meaningful input.
8. Output might play a role in providing input to someone else. There is no evidence that output practice affects our implicit language developing system. However, it might facilitate the development of a skill.

## Implications for Language Teaching

1. Communication cannot be equated to Q/A. Communication is the interpretation, expression and negotiation of meaning in a given context for a specific purpose.
2. Comprehensible and meaningful input are the key ingredients for language learning. Non-traditional and interactive listening and reading tasks can provide input for acquisition.
3. Explicit information makes no difference and it is not input for learning.
4. Vocabulary is learned through input and by making form-meaning connections. Repetition and memorization do not work. Learners should be given opportunities to process new words. vocabulary learning and teaching should consider the following: (1) present new words frequently and repeatedly in the input, (2) use meaning-bearing comprehensible input when presenting new words, (3) limit forced output during the initial stages of learning new words, (4) limit forced semantic elaboration during the initial stages of learning new words, (5) progress from less demanding to more demanding vocabulary-related activities.
5. An explanation of grammar and mechanical practice (use of drills) is not conducive to language learning. Learners do not acquire languages through imitation and repetition. The language system is not affected by learning the explicit rules of a target language. Drills do not foster language learning. A focus on focus should be input-oriented and

meaningful-based. Learners should be encouraged to make accurate form-meaning mappings. Grammar teaching should focus on both form and meaning and output practice should follow input practice.
6. Explicit corrective feedback provides learners with a meta-linguistic explanation or explicit error correction. This kind of direct error correction might have a temporary effect (improve performance) but does little good in the long run (it does not cause a change in learners' implicit system). Corrective feedback should be indirect and implicit and should result in uptake. Implicit corrective feedback indirectly and incidentally informs learners of their non-target-like use of certain linguistic features. Recasts, confirmation checks, clarification requests and even paralinguistic signs such as facial expressions can all constitute implicit corrective feedback and might have a facilitative effect.
7. Mechanical output practice makes no difference and it does not lead to language acquisition. Output in the form of interaction is the language produced by learners that has a communicative purpose and is produced for a specific meaning. Communicative and interactive tasks (e.g. interactive speaking tasks, process-oriented written tasks, interactive reading comprehension tasks, listening active tasks) can facilitate language learning. Language learners benefit a great deal from exposure to comprehensible input, conversational interaction and opportunities for the negotiation of meaning.
8. Language tasks are the backbone of language instruction as they encourage interaction and negotiation of meaning.

# Is There an Effective Way to Teach Grammar in the Classroom?

There has been a dramatic shift from traditional grammar-oriented methods to more communicative grammar approaches. This shift has meant a change in the way grammar is taught and practised in the language classroom. In traditional methods, grammar was provided through long and elaborated explanations of the grammatical rules of the target language. Explanations of those grammatical rules were provided and followed by output-based practice (written and oral exercises) where the main focus was to practise the grammatical rules to obtain accuracy. Traditional grammar instruction practice is usually provided following a particular sequence which goes from mechanical to communicative drills practice. Most books used in the UK and across Europe to teach foreign languages approach the teaching of grammar in a very traditional way. The grammar section of these books is generally characterized by rules and explanations of forms and grammatical principles using learners' first language. The explanation is followed by pattern practice and substitution drills. Real-life situations are completely ignored and practice is implemented in a completely decontextualized way. This is not the way we acquire a second language, and imitation and repetition play very little role in language learning. Research in language learning has also shown that traditional approaches to grammar instruction which involve the use of drills don't foster language learning.

The question addressed here is whether there are certain types of grammar teaching better than others and whether they could be incorporated successfully into the teaching of a second language. The question is not whether or not we should teach grammar, but rather how and what we should teach.

First of all, we must emphasize that the theoretical and empirical findings in L2 research have on one hand indicated the limited role of grammar teaching (e.g. instruction cannot alter the route of acquisition), and on the other hand, highlighted the importance of incorporating grammar in a more communicative framework of language teaching by devising grammar tasks that enhance the grammatical features in the input. The question is to determine what type of grammar is more successful in terms of helping learners internalize the grammatical features of a target language. Learners bring to the task of learning a language, a variety of internal mechanisms and traits that effectively override most instructional efforts. However, the more researchers learn about what learners do with input and how they do it, the closer they come to understanding the possibilities of instructional effects. Such research insights have driven researchers to examine the effects not of instruction more generally, but of particular kinds of instructional interventions – those that were both input-oriented and meaning-based. These interventions, which aim at manipulating the input learners receive, include approaches such as text enhancement, structured input and input flood. When selecting the types of grammar instruction techniques we should take into consideration the nature of the target form.

Therefore to go back to our original question: Are there types of instruction better than others? We must say that there is not one particular type of grammar instruction approach better than others. However, we must emphasize again that effective types of grammar instruction share a common and essential ingredient: input. To develop effective grammar tasks, language teachers should ensure that input is manipulated so to facilitate grammar learning. Learners should be encouraged to make accurate form-meaning mappings. Grammar tasks should focus on both form and meaning, and output practice should follow input practice. Finally, we have emphasized the importance to use a variety of grammar tasks and the necessity for language instructors to use an eclectic approach to grammar instruction. One size does not fit all.

# Are Particular Types of Error Correction Better Than Others?

The role of error correction (corrective feedback is the term we used) has been widely debated ins L2 learning, spawning a great deal of theoretical and empirical research. The role of corrective feedback in language learning is not clear yet. Research on corrective feedback has attempted to prove that corrective feedback exists, it is usable and it is used, and it is necessary. Explicit corrective feedback provides learners with explicit error correction. This kind of direct error correction might have a temporary effect (improve performance) but does little good in the long run (it does not cause a change in learners' underlying implicit system). Implicit corrective feedback indirectly and incidentally informs learners of their non-target-like use of certain linguistic features. Recasts, confirmation checks, clarification requests, repetitions and even paralinguistic signs such as facial expressions can all constitute indirect correction techniques. Implicit corrective feedback (e.g. confirmation checks, clarification requests and recasts) aims at inducing learners to detect a discrepancy between their interlanguage and the target language. Indirect correction techniques can be further classified into two types: (1) Recasts that provide the correct form immediately after learner errors and (2) repair techniques (e.g. clarification requests, elicitations) do not provide target-like forms. Instead, they promote learners to repair their errors by themselves by providing a chance to reformulate their previous ill-formed utterances. The question is: which is the type of indirect correction that can be the most beneficial in language learning and teaching? The answer is that the two main types of indirect error correction do different things. Repair support suggests that this kind of corrective feedback can assist learners in actively confronting errors in ways that may lead to revisions of their hypotheses about the target language. Support for recast suggests that it might enable learners to be exposed to target forms and elicit repetition, and this repetition may, in turn, enhance salience. Enhanced input may also contribute to the acquisition of new linguistic forms. In addition, as claimed previously, learners may be able to juxtapose incorrect and correct forms through recasts and eventually notice the gap in their knowledge. Language teachers might adopt an eclectic approach to error correction considering a series of factors such as the form and the learners' proficiency level. The readiness of learners to overcome certain errors must be taken into account. If learners are not ready to process a certain feature because they have not reached that stage, not even corrective feedback will be helpful. Effective corrective feedback techniques are the ones that seem to produce student-generated repairs. Language teachers should encourage learners to self-correct and they should provide appropriate cues for the learner to self-repair.

# Is There an Effective Way to Teach Language Skills (Listening, Reading, Speaking, Writing) in the Classroom?

In the present teaching textbook, we have argued that language teaching should move from input practice to output practice. Learning a language is intake-dependent and teachers would need to provide learners with opportunities to make correct form-meaning connections in the input they are exposed to. Once learners have processed language correctly, we should provide an opportunity for learners to use the target language for communicative purposes. Output is the language produced by learners that has a communicative purpose and is produced for a specific meaning. Oral communicative practice is in antithesis with a traditional oral practice largely used in a traditional textbook. In traditional speaking tasks, learners are asked to look at some pictures or dialogue and then perform that dialogue following a specific pattern. Based on what we have said in the textbook, we have developed a series of guidelines language teachers should follow in developing effective speaking tasks. Speaking tasks should be designed to allow language teachers and learners to interact with each other. The role of the teacher is to design the task (planner) and encourage participation and contribution from learners (co-workers). The learner's role is to share responsibility in interaction and task completion. By providing a series of tasks to complete we encourage learners to take responsibility for generating the information themselves rather than just receiving it. Language teachers should develop speaking tasks in which learners are provided with opportunities to speak the target language at all times in a rich environment that contains collaborative work, authentic materials and tasks in which they share knowledge by interacting with each other. The ability to communicate in a second language clearly and efficiently contributes to the overall success in the learning of a second language. Therefore, language teachers must pay greater attention to the development of speaking skills. Rather than leading learners to pure memorization, they should provide learners with a rich environment where meaningful communication takes place. With this aim in mind, various speaking tasks such as those presented in this textbook can greatly contribute to developing learners' communicative competence necessary to learn a second language.

Writing is a cognitive process that involves a series of sub-processes. Writing is a process where learners explore, consolidate and develop rhetorical objectives. The same definition used for communication applies to the written language. We express ourselves both in speaking and writing. When we write a grocery list, for example, we accomplish an act of communication. Traditional writing tasks do not achieve this. When designing a writing activity for learners, language teachers should take into consideration the mental processes that comprise the act of communication (expression, interpretation and negotiation of meaning in a given context and for a specific purpose). In doing so, they would encourage learners (step-by-step approach to the written task) to work together to generate content, select a purpose, plan and organize the composition (pre-writing activities) and eventually review and evaluate (content and form) their composition.

Reading/comprehension task is also an important component of a communicative language classroom. Our proposed reading comprehension framework challenge directly the way reading is done in traditional approaches (translation and answering questions). When designing a reading comprehension task we should take into account the processes responsible for reading comprehension and should develop a step-by-step approach (from pre-reading to personalization) similar to the one used for writing.

Reading activities in traditional textbooks consist mainly of two types: translation tasks (read a passage and translate it); and answering questions from a text (a typical task/exercise is: Read the dialogue/text and answer the following questions). Reading should be viewed as 'reading in another language rather than as an exercise in translation'. The fact that language learners do not necessarily have the verbal virtuosity of a native reader means instructors need to use some strategies to help them. The framework presented here takes into consideration the need to guide learners in their comprehension of a text. Developing reading comprehension skills involves the interaction of a variety of knowledge sources. In Chapter 6 we have proposed an interactive model to develop learners' reading skills. Specific guidelines have been suggested for language teachers to follow. Reading comprehension tasks should be developed to stimulate learners' motivation and should have specific communicative purposes and goals. A five-stage approach should be followed in designing reading comprehension tasks. The pre-reading stage is to prepare students for reading and activating their background knowledge. The reading stage is to help learners to read the text and scan for specific information or meanings. The text-interaction reading task stage is to gradually bridge the gap between the text and the reader. The post-reading stage is to check and verify learners' comprehension. The personalization stage is to help learners to exploit the communicative function of the text through the use of various tasks (e.g. solve a problem, create a poster, apply main concepts to another context and related key issues to a different context).

One particularly important part of language teaching is to help students develop their competence to listen for a specific purpose. To develop learners' listening skills, instructors should provide some tasks which reflect listening situations occurring outside the classroom. Learners should be guided to the task of listening in terms of what meanings they should expect from the passage. At the same time, learners must be able to (take responsibility) extract the main content/information from the text. The role of comprehensible input and conversational interaction has assumed greater importance in L2 teaching as learners benefit a great deal from exposure to comprehensible input, conversational interaction and opportunities for negotiation of meaning. Listening is not just a bottom-up process where learners hear sounds and need to decode those sounds from the smaller units to large texts, but it is also a top-down process where learners reconstruct the original meaning of the speaker using incoming sounds as clues. In this reconstruction process, the listener uses prior knowledge of the context and situation within which the listening takes place to make sense of what he or she hears. Listeners use a series of mental processes and prior knowledge sources to understand and interpret what they hear. Listening is a very active skill given that learners are actively engaged in different processes while they are exposed to aural stimuli. We can distinguish between three main processes: perceiving, attending and assigning meaning. Now if we look at listening in the language classroom the two main questions to be asked are: What kind of listening tasks are learners engaged in the classroom? Do they have the opportunity to develop their skills and strategies? The challenge is to develop listening tasks that will stimulate the development of listening skills while equipping them with listening strategies.

When teachers develop listening tasks they should take the following steps:

1. They should expose listeners to comprehensible input;
2. They should use the target language to conduct business;
3. They should allow learners to nominate topics and structure the discourse. Learners are much more likely to get involved and become active listeners and participants;
4. They should develop a listening task for a specific communicative purpose;
5. They should respond to the learner as a listener, not an instructor;
6. They should provide some good listening gambits to learners. In addition to simply allowing more opportunities for collaborative listening, instructors can also point out learners' typical listening gambits for signalling non-understanding, confirmation and so forth.

In the pre-listening stage, language teachers should set the context, create motivation and activate learners' prior knowledge through cooperative learning tasks (e.g. brainstorming, think-pair-share). Pre-listening tasks include vocabulary learning and/or identifying key ideas contained in the upcoming input. In the while-listening stage, tasks require learners to listen for main ideas to establish the context and transfer information. Learners are exposed to listening bottom-up tasks (e.g. word sentence recognition, listening for the different morphological endings), top-down tasks (identifying the topic, understanding the meaning of the sentence) and interactive tasks (e.g. listening to a list and categorizing the words, following directions). Main listening tasks at this stage include guided note-taking, and completion of a picture or schematic diagram or table. Finally, in the post-listening stage learners examine the functional language and infer the meaning of vocabulary (e.g. guess the meaning of unknown vocabulary, analyse the success of communication in the script, brainstorm alternative ways of expression). In the final stage of a listening comprehension task, language learners are given post-listening tasks that involve additional reading, writing, speaking and interactive activities.

# Is There a Particular Effective Methodology to Teach Language in the Classroom?

Language teachers are always interested in finding out what is the best way to teach languages. In the past many years, we have witnessed a variety of methods in language teaching (e.g. Grammar Translation, Audiolingual, Communicative Language Teaching and Task-Based, among others). Language teachers should not look at the 'right method' to teach languages, as there is not just one. They should instead talk about a principled and evidence-based approach to language teaching which should be drawn from principles, theories and research in L2 learning and develop a specific definition of what language is. Language teachers are encouraged to take suggestions from here and there when it comes to pedagogical issues, as long as what they choose is guided and informed by theory and empirical research in language learning and teaching. In this textbook, it has been argued for a learner-centred type of language teaching, where learners engage in communicative and effective tasks which involve group work and interaction with other learners. A teaching environment is one in which learners are exposed to tasks for a specific purpose and where the teacher is in the position to give the students many opportunities for spontaneous production, interaction and negotiation of meaning; in short, a language classroom is where learners should receive comprehensible input and be given opportunities to interact with their peers. A different role for the language teacher has been proposed, one that creates the opportunity and the conditions in the classroom for L2 learners to co-participate and take responsibility for their learning. In this new environment, learning can take place naturally and teaching can be effective. In this teaching and learning environment, meaning is emphasized over form, and the amount of correction is kept to a minimum, letting the students express themselves and self-repair. Comprehensible, simplified and message-based input is provided through the use of contextual props, cues and gestures rather than structural grading. A variety of task discourse types are introduced where learners engage in real communication. Based on our discussion in this textbook, a principle and evidence-based approach to L2 teaching is proposed. The main tenets of this approach are to:

1. ensure that learners are exposed to extensive 'good quality' input.
2. ensure that learners engage with language where meaning is emphasized over form;
3. ensure that learners are exposed to a focus on the form which helps them to make accurate form-meaning connections;
4. ensure that the amount of error correction is kept to a minimum, and learners are encouraged to self-repair;
5. ensure that learners are exposed to language tasks when they have the opportunity to interact with each other, exchange information and negotiate meaning;
6. ensure that learners have opportunities to develop communicative competence and to use language for communicative purposes.

# Second Language Teacher Education Programme: Evaluation Form

Participant's Name (optional): _____

Please indicate your rating of the presentation in the categories below by circling the appropriate number, using a scale of 1 to 5 (5 = completely; 4 = to a high degree; 3 = moderately; 2 = minimally; 1 = not at all).

**OBJECTIVES**

| | |
|---|---|
| 1. The programme met the stated objectives | 1  2  3  4  5 |
| 2. The programme met my needs | 1  2  3  4  5 |
| 3. Length of the programme was adequate | 1  2  3  4  5 |

**TEACHER**

| | |
|---|---|
| 1. Knowledgeable in content areas | 1  2  3  4  5 |
| 2. Content consistent with objectives | 1  2  3  4  5 |
| 3. Clarified content in response to questions | 1  2  3  4  5 |

**CONTENT**

| | |
|---|---|
| 1. Content was appropriate | 1  2  3  4  5 |
| 2. Consistent with stated objectives | 1  2  3  4  5 |
| 3. Content was presented clearly | 1  2  3  4  5 |

**TEACHING METHODS**

| | | | | | |
|---|---|---|---|---|---|
| 1. Visual aids, handouts, and presentations clarified content | 1 | 2 | 3 | 4 | 5 |
| 2. Teaching methods were appropriate | 1 | 2 | 3 | 4 | 5 |
| 3. Teaching style was effective | 1 | 2 | 3 | 4 | 5 |

**RELEVANCY**

| | | | | | |
|---|---|---|---|---|---|
| 1. Information could be applied to practice | 1 | 2 | 3 | 4 | 5 |
| 2. Information could contribute to achieving professional development | 1 | 2 | 3 | 4 | 5 |

**LIKES AND DISLIKES**

| | | | | | |
|---|---|---|---|---|---|
| 1. What did you like most about the programme? | 1 | 2 | 3 | 4 | 5 |
| 2. What specific things did you like least about the programme? | 1 | 2 | 3 | 4 | 5 |
| 3. If the programme was repeated, what should be left out or changed? | 1 | 2 | 3 | 4 | 5 |

# Index

Audiolingual Method 7, 55, 70, 89, 220

behaviourism 7, 71, 80, 88

Computer-Assisted Language Learning 197, 201–4
Computer-Mediated Communication 197, 201, 203
communicative/communicative approach 8–9, 55, 71–2, 75, 82, 106, 108, 112, 116–17, 121, 123, 128–30, 133, 151, 157, 164, 167–8, 174–5, 194, 200, 208, 213–14, 216–18, 220–1
communicative value 28, 40
competence 3, 13, 31–4, 38–40, 50, 64, 99, 103–4, 117, 119–20, 122–3, 126, 130, 140, 161, 173–4, 179–80, 194, 203, 217–18, 221
corrective feedback 3, 18, 48, 50, 102, 109–10, 132, 156–64, 170, 196, 200–2, 213, 215–16

elicitation 131, 158–62, 215
explicit knowledge 4, 15–16, 23–4, 29–34, 39, 49–50, 55, 59, 63–4, 66–7, 98, 156, 209–10

focus on form 44–5, 50–2, 66, 70–2, 81–2, 94–5, 103–4, 108–9, 120–2, 125, 131, 133–4, 138–40, 145, 147–56
form (word)-meaning connections 4, 9, 12–13, 31, 43, 45, 47, 57–9, 65–6, 80–1, 100, 138–40, 144–5, 148, 150, 153, 155, 180–1, 200–1, 212, 216, 221
frequency 13, 20, 31, 82, 96, 100, 109–10, 145, 147, 154

Grammar Translation Method 55, 70, 89, 220

implicit knowledge 2, 9, 13, 23–4, 29–34, 39–40, 49, 59, 63–4, 66–7, 170, 209–10
input/comprenesible/meaningful 2–7, 9–11, 13–22, 24, 26, 30–4, 37–40, 42–50, 52, 55, 58–9, 61, 64, 66, 71, 80–8, 91–110, 119, 128, 131, 133–4, 139–42, 144–5, 147–62, 170, 172–3, 179, 194, 199, 201–3, 209, 212–16, 218–21
input enhancement 44–5, 66, 81–2, 144–6, 150, 152–6, 164, 214
input flood 34, 82, 144–5, 147–8, 151–5, 214
intake 7, 9, 11–12, 18–21, 30, 99, 108, 138, 140, 155, 201, 211, 216
interaction 3–4, 9, 14, 22, 25, 32–40, 45, 47–51, 57–8, 68, 71–2, 76, 91–2, 95–7, 99–105, 108–10, 112–14, 119, 121, 129, 156–60, 163–4, 168–9, 173–4, 182–5, 192, 194–6, 201–3, 213, 217–19, 220
input processing 9, 12–13, 19, 21–2, 30, 32–3, 40, 43–5, 47, 49, 80–5, 87, 94–6, 99–100, 103, 105, 119, 139–40, 143–4, 150, 153–4, 164, 169, 171–2, 174, 180, 211

lexicon 10, 21, 57, 68, 81, 88, 128

motivation 41, 47–48, 52, 104, 199, 202–3, 205, 218–19
morphology 10, 21, 58, 68, 88, 162

negotiation of meaning 14, 36, 49, 52, 71, 73, 76, 79, 95, 101–2, 104, 109, 112–14, 127, 157–9, 162, 169–70, 196, 201, 212–13, 217–18, 220
noticing 40, 43, 128, 144–5, 154, 195

output 7, 23–4, 26, 30, 35–40, 45, 47, 49–50, 81, 85, 87, 108, 110, 118–20, 127–8, 131, 138–9, 148–52, 155–6, 158–61, 169–70, 198, 200, 210–13, 215–16 output processing 26, 40

parameter 16–17, 21, 59
phonology 10, 21, 57–8
poverty of the stimulus 15, 21

recast 50, 158–60, 163, 170, 213, 215–16
redundant 28, 145, 153, 165

structured input 66, 139–43, 146, 149–55, 169, 174, 214
structured output 120, 149–52, 155

syntax 7, 10, 20–1, 39, 57–8, 68, 97–8, 119, 123

task-based approach 128–30, 194, 200, 220
textual enhancement 44, 66, 144–6, 150, 152–5, 214

Universal Grammar 17, 19, 21, 25, 212

working memory 12, 22, 140, 165